THE
PROPHECY

THE PROPHECY

Eternity Unfolds

WILLIAM AYLES

© 2003 by William Ayles. All rights reserved.

TIMELINE INTERNATIONAL is a research group dedicated to the methodical exploration and dynamic presentation of the inherent accuracy and integrity of the Word of God.

No part of this publication may be reproduced, stored in a retrieval system, or transmitted in any way by any means, electronic, mechanical, photocopy, recording, or otherwise, without the prior permission of the copyright holder except as provided by USA copyright law.

All scriptures are taken from the Holy Bible, New International Version, Copyright © 1973, 1978, 1984 by the International Bible Society. Used by permission of Zondervan Publishing House. The "NIV" and "New International Version" trademarks are registered in the United States Patent and Trademark Office by International Bible Society.

Scriptures references marked KJV are taken from the King James Version of the Bible.

ISBN 1-57921-464-9
Library of Congress Catalog Card Number: 2002104799

If the doors of perception were cleansed every thing would appear to man as it is: infinite.

—William Blake

Contents

AUTHOR'S NOTE 9

PROLOGUE: *Creation: Theory and Prophecy* 21

ACT ONE
1. *Spiritual Warfare* 49
2. *Events of the End: The Seven Seals of Christ's Prophecy* 79
3. *The Seventieth "Seven"* 139
4. *The Code of Psalms* 151

ACT TWO
5. *The Doors of Paradise* 189
6. *The Divine Sign* 207
7. *The Living Temple of the Living God* 233
8. *Crowns and Glory* 249

EPILOGUE: *Modern-day Psalms* 261

NOTES 269

PSALM 103 291

ACKNOWLEDGMENTS 295

Author's Note

Were it not for divine inspiration, this book never would have been written.

Imagine a world where everything you take for granted is no more. Imagine how you would feel if you woke up one morning and the world you knew the night before was over? That world shall be this world—before this decade is out. Divine intervention shall affect the course of human existence, and the future will be forever altered.

I submit to you that why "you" are here on Earth, and what waits in your future, cannot only be known, but also can be known with an unwavering, divine assurance. It is in this manner that what lies ahead for this world need not be feared but embraced.

It was on February 24, 2000, a Thursday night around 8:20 P.M., when my life crossed a threshold and I awoke to a new perception of this physical reality on Earth. That night marked the start of an odyssey that spanned six weeks—none of the "events" that followed could be scientifically explained.

That Thursday night, I was lying on the couch watching a public television show on Stonehenge (a stone structure in England that is understood to be an ancient religious site). I had recently returned from a business trip and simply wanted to relax in front of the tube. I settled in for an interesting hour of fascinating information.

Twenty minutes into the show the narrator was offering various ideas as to who actually built this stone structure, questioning when it could have been built. At that precise moment—out of nowhere—energy began to flood my mind. It was as if I was a receiver of energy waves, and someone had just thrown the switch. I felt "alive" with a sense of inner rejuvenation. Thoughts about Heaven and Earth—creation itself—filled my mind; the pictures just poured forth. Within the hour, I called a trusted friend and poured the same intensity over the phone, elaborating on how this (ongoing) energy had already sparked a series of intriguing thoughts.

The following evening, I visited the same friend, and in the midst of recounting the occurrence, I thought about how the energy coincided with Stonehenge (and who built it). At that moment, a thought came to me: "generations of old." Immediately, I was inspired to find where "generations of old" appeared in the Bible. After referring to my concordance, I turned to a verse that was unfamiliar to me: Isaiah 51:9. This is what I read: "Awake, awake, put on strength, O arm of the Lord; awake, as in the ancient days, in the generations of old." After reading on to the next verse, I snapped to attention and soon began walking around the living room, holding my head in shock and awe.

I hadn't yet broken my stride, when I saw a picture in my mind and spoke out loud: "Eight white tiles." As I sat back down to continue reading, I read a total of eight verses: Isaiah 51:9–16 (KJV). Clearly, the picture in my mind of eight tiles (along with what occurred the night before) was *revelation*: divine energy that imparts knowledge. (Just as our own brain waves produce thoughts, so do energy waves that are of divine origin.)

This mind picture of eight tiles directed me to read eight verses. Incredibly, these eight verses are uniquely placed in that chapter, marking a defined section of Scripture that unmistakably identifies the spiritual warfare between God and his enemy Satan, and the role that God's human creation plays in that war. As I read through the verses, I arrived at the apex, verse 16: "And I have put my words in thy mouth, and I have covered thee in the shadow of mine hand, that I may plant the heavens, and lay the foundations of the earth, and say unto Zion, Thou *art* my people."

This first twenty-four hours of divine intervention became the catalyst for me to resume my research of the Bible, building upon a study that commenced twenty years earlier. Over the next six weeks, Heaven guided my steps by revelation. Into my thought patterns went information—knowledge and wisdom.

It was like viewing life through a kaleidoscope: the light of God was within and I saw visions, seeing life from a perspective that words alone cannot produce. In the visions, I could see what was occurring in the spiritual world—in real time. In other words, we are not alone in this physical realm that we occupy; just as there is forward progress made in the physical world, there is forward progress made in the spiritual world. This forward progress in the spiritual realm—as it applies to *right now*—is made clear in the chapters that follow.

Through all of this, I could sense the Creator's hand on my life showing me that I was to exit the corporate world and prepare to write this book: a book that would reveal the essence of what I was shown (in the spiritual realm), and, in addition, a book that would reveal the truest, purest intention of spirituality, and how that spirituality empowers us to arrive at a new place—in this life and in the next.

I submit to you that what awaits in this book is what the Lord God put in my mouth, so that our generation on Earth may be informed of its future, and that *you* may have the knowledge necessary to participate in divine prophecy.

Central to this thought is the focal point of this book: the code of Psalms. It is the biblical code that weaves together time and prophecy, revealing when the prophecies found in the Book of Revelation, and those given by the angel Gabriel to the prophet Daniel, shall be fulfilled. I enter into this undertaking with the greatest gravity, cognizant of its dramatic nature.

By the grace of Heaven, the code—this mathematical phenomenon—is now unveiled. It reveals that we are rapidly closing in on the fulfillment of prophecy—the future is moving ever closer to the present.

Here, at the dawn of the twenty-first century, we are well aware that the world has been jolted into a new sense of apprehension—a new threat from those who seek to destabilize peace and prosperity. This undercurrent of evil that encompasses the globe and fuels the tension between peoples and nations is undeniable. What I present in the following chapters is that the source of this undercurrent is also undeniable: spirit.

In essence, both good and evil—ever-present in this world—have a spiritual source, and on *this* planet, the battle between the two is being waged. This conflict shall continue forward, accelerating toward an unprecedented clash that will forever alter the course of history.

All of my adult life I have sought to understand the cause behind the effect: why life is the way it is—its purpose and its ultimate finish. Early on, I sought to understand my place in time and desired to know what happens after breathing my last. Questions of this nature ran deep within, and when they surfaced, I sought the truth. I submit to you that I have been given a treasure chest of knowledge—the truth that caused my heart to glow and liberated my mind from the universal fear: the fear of death. I want you to experience the same freedom.

This said, *The Prophecy* begins with a presentation on creation. The Prologue presents recent scientific evidence, and reaches back in time to the ancient writings of the biblical prophets. This compilation of thought casts a long shadow on existing theories that seek to explain the origin of life. Conversely, scientific evidence is seen to be in alignment with the ancient texts—which convey not only the origin of life but also its destiny.

In the first act of the book, you are introduced to the relationship between the spiritual war on this planet and the human soul. Act One is intended to open a new dimension of thought—a new consciousness of our

Author's Note

oneness with the will of Heaven. Pursuing this thought, Heaven's prophecy for Earth is then placed on a time continuum.

Essential to this discussion on prophecy is the Book of Revelation. It is the only book of the Bible that marks end-time prophecies with a numbered sequence, and by doing so establishes the framework for understanding the chronological order of end-time events. All pieces of the end-time prophetic puzzle given throughout the Old and New Testaments fit into the Revelation framework.

In accordance with this, Act One presents the numbered progression of "final" events, incorporating additional prophecies from a number of biblical prophets—enhancing the prophetic picture. Intricately linked to this picture is the prophecy given by the angel Gabriel. It reveals a world that is living within a defined amount of time, and how divine intervention shall initiate a new kingdom on this Earth. It is against this backdrop of divine prophecy that the code of Psalms is unlocked, marking prophecy and time.

In Act Two, you are introduced to the realm of divine revelation as it applies to eternal life. The focus of Act Two is your personal destiny: you will know how to attain a life that has no end. You will understand the spiritual nature of a fulfilled life in this world, where you can know beyond all doubt that eternal life is yours, and that you will live to see God.

Banish doubt; dissolve anxiety; know calm.

If you ever felt that there was to be more to your life, you are right. In the Epilogue, you will find thoughts of modern-day poets; expect to expand the way you know God. Trade in the world's blinders for Heaven's awareness: see yourself as Heaven does, and see life through the eyes of God. Walk into the vision of who you were created to be: the fullness of your personality energized by divine love.

I invite you to immerse yourself in the words of prophets, theologians, scientists, and poets. Collectively, they reveal a picture that paints answers to life's mysteries—their expressions of reality let you walk through a door of understanding that will forever positively affect your soul.

Prologue

CREATION: THEORY AND PROPHECY

> Not everything that can be counted counts, and not everything that counts can be counted.
> —Albert Einstein

When it comes to explaining the origin of life, no two theories are more opposed to each other than "creation" and "evolution." Whereas creationists believe that supernatural intelligence created life as we know it, evolutionists contend that life originated from single-cell organisms, which evolved into modern-day species. Hence, together, the two theories give us the opposites:

> Creation and evolution, between them, exhaust the possible explanations for the origin of living things. Organisms either appeared on the earth fully developed or they did not. If they did not, they must have developed from pre-existing species by some process of modification. If they did appear in a fully developed state, they must have been created by some omnipotent intelligence.[1]

Charles Darwin promoted the idea that omnipotent intelligence played no role in man's creation, and "it was because Darwinian theory broke man's link with God and set him adrift in a cosmos without purpose or end that its impact was so fundamental. No other intellectual revolution in modern times

Creation: Theory and Prophecy 23

... so profoundly affected the way men viewed themselves and their place in the universe."[2]

In the year 1838, Charles Darwin lit the match that gave birth to evolutionary theory. In that year, he recorded the following statement in his notes: "Man in his arrogance thinks himself a great work. worthy [sic] the interposition of a deity, more humble & I believe true to consider him created from animals."[3]

Darwin held to the belief that man's arrogance produced creation theory. He contended that it was much more reasonable to assume that mankind evolved into its current state. In his book titled *The Origin of Species*, Darwin stated: "I should infer ... that probably all the organic beings which have ever lived on this earth have descended from some one primordial form, into which life was first breathed."[4] According to Darwin, the unbroken chain of life extended back millions of years, and artifacts of prehistoric man presumably represented man's ancestral roots.

Whereas Darwin claimed a connection between modern man and antiquity, the prophets of God spoke of a separation. In the Book of Genesis, for example, Moses said that life did exist before modern man but that it was not connected to him. In his writings, Moses spoke of a "void" that preceded the creation of mankind:

> In the beginning God created the heaven and the earth. And the earth . . . [became[5]] without form, and void; and darkness *was* upon the face of the deep. And the Spirit of God moved upon the face of the waters. . . . [And] God created man in his *own* image, in the image of God created he him; male and female created he them. (Gen. 1:1, 2, 27 KJV)

In the beginning, when God created Heaven and Earth, he furnished both areas with life. However, once darkness encased the planet, Earth could no longer sustain flesh and blood. Thereby, a world that once teemed with life *became* void of it. It was following this void that the Spirit of God re-infused life back into the planet, bringing about the current kingdom of modern man. Herein, man would "replenish the earth" (Gen. 1:28 KJV). This revelation given by Moses is in direct contradiction to Darwin's theory, which states that man was not replenishing an empty Earth but was an extension of life's earliest beginnings.

With the theory of evolution diametrically opposed to creationism, the obvious question arises as to whether scientific evidence ever supported either position. Do fossils demonstrate an evolution of or a creation of a species? This issue was addressed by a biochemist named D. B. Gower. In his article titled "Scientist Rejects Evolution," Gower cited material evidence when he stated that fully developed species appeared at given points in time—all along the time continuum. Gower wrote:

> The creation account in Genesis and the theory of evolution could not be reconciled. One must be right and the other wrong. The story of the fossils agreed with the account of Genesis. In the oldest rocks we did not find a series of fos-

sils covering the gradual changes from the most primitive creatures to developed forms, but rather in the oldest rocks developed species suddenly appeared. Between every species there was a complete absence of intermediate fossils.[6]

Fossilized evidence supports the instantaneous appearance of various creations. It does not support an ongoing evolution within a unified creation.

Even those who subscribe to Darwinian theory acknowledge how recent scientific evidence is causing a reexamination of the fundamental assumptions of Darwin. As a director of a large graduate program in biology stated:

> I personally hold the evolutionary position, but yet lament the fact that the majority of our Ph.D. graduates are frightfully ignorant of many of the serious problems of the evolution theory. These problems will not be solved unless we bring them to the attention of

students. Most students assume evolution is proved, the missing link is found, and all we have left is a few rough edges to smooth out. Actually, quite the contrary is true; and many recent discoveries . . . have forced us to re-evaluate our basic assumptions.[7]

Even with all the research conducted in the twentieth century, a scientific link between mankind and another species never materialized. Michael Denton, an Australian molecular biologist, addressed this ongoing issue of evidence in his 1986 book *Evolution: A Theory in Crisis*:

> The fact is that the evidence was so patchy one hundred years ago that even Darwin himself had increasing doubts as to the validity of his views, and the only aspect of his theory which has received any support over the past century is where it applies to microevolutionary phenomena. His general theory, that all life on earth had originated and evolved by a gradual successive accumulation of

> fortuitous mutations, is still, as it was in Darwin's time, a highly speculative hypothesis entirely without direct factual support.[8]

Although Darwin's theory of evolution finds support on a microlevel (evolution occurring within a given species), Darwin's general theory—that man evolved from an entirely different species—remains a "highly speculative hypothesis." Even Darwin himself lamented late in his life that no evidence had surfaced to prove his theory correct.

Emerging evidence continues to reveal a picture other than what Darwin painted. Late in the twentieth century, a group of German and American scientists extracted DNA from the bone of a Neandertal man. (Neandertals lived between 300,000 B.C. and 30,000 B.C. in the Middle East, Western Asia, and Europe.) The scientific team compared Neandertal DNA to that of modern man, and found that the Neandertal sequence fell well outside the range of variation found in (our) humankind. Dr. Mark Stoneking, associate

Creation: Theory and Prophecy 29

professor of anthropology at Penn State, stated: "These results indicate that Neandertals did not contribute mitochondrial DNA to modern humans. . . . Neandertals are not our ancestors."[9]

No scientist on Earth can definitively state that life within modern man is absolutely linked to other preexisting life-forms. To draw such a conclusion from existing evidence would be an unthinkable departure from the "scientific method," for in applying this approach, a valid conclusion demands unmistakable evidence linking cause and effect. Michael J. Behe, associate professor of biochemistry at Lehigh University and author of *Darwin's Black Box: The Biochemical Challenge to Evolution*, addressed the issue of causation in the following manner:

> "Evolution" . . . implies that random mutation and natural selection powered the changes in life. The idea is that just by chance an animal was born that was slightly faster or stronger than its siblings. Its descendants inherited the

> change and eventually won the contest of survival over the descendants of other members of the species. Over time, repetition of the process resulted in great changes—and, indeed, wholly different animals. That's the theory. A practical difficulty, however, is that one can't test the theory from fossils.[10]

Adding to the dilemma, Darwin openly acknowledged his need to transcend classic scientific boundaries in order to produce his evolutionary conclusion. In a letter to a Harvard biology professor, Darwin wrote: "I am quite conscious that my speculations run beyond the bounds of true science."[11]

This position held by Darwin is clearly understood in light of the observation made by British scientist L. Merson Davies: "It has been estimated that no fewer than 800 phrases in the subjunctive mood (such as '*Let us assume*,' or '*We may well suppose*,' etc.) are to be found between the covers of Darwin's *Origin of Species* alone."[12] Without question, this approach produced an unsettling effect on objectivity. As stated by Dr. Colin Patterson, senior paleontologist at the British Museum of Natural History:

> There is much in current day Darwinian conclusion which is based on "circular reasoning" (i.e. is tautologous) and in fact much of the information is exactly contrary to reality, a mistaking of "cause" for "effect" ("inverse reasoning" in terms of logic). For example, evolutionists generally consider "Natural Selection" to be the "cause" of evolution; in fact, if it is anything at all, it is the cause of only one thing, survival of organisms. In other words, it would be an "effect" of evolution, not a "cause" of it.[13]

Ironically, although scientists and prophets disagree with Darwin's *conclusions*, they agree with his *observations*. For example, Darwin observed, "when a species has vanished from the face of the earth, the same form never reappears."[14] This observation agrees with creation theory. Once a species is extinct, it cannot regenerate itself.

Evolutionists contend that extinction occurs when a species evolves out of existence; when the evolutionary cycle is complete, the species simply ceases to exist. In contrast, creationists state that a species doesn't evolve out of existence but rather dies out of existence. Extinction comes by way of the death of an entire life-form. A species ceases to exist because the seed that produced that species died with it. Like the dinosaur kingdom, which went into decline some sixty-five million years ago, no extinct kingdoms of life have ever reappeared. Without seed, there is no possibility of life.

No conflict exists between creationists and Darwin's view about the regeneration of life. It is only with Darwin's conclusion that the prophets and scientific evidence disagree.

The conclusion—that modern man is the product of lower intelligence—excludes the need for the existence of higher intelligence. Darwinian theorists need irrefutable evidence in order to believe in a supernatural creator. The irony is that the same theorists

Creation: Theory and Prophecy 33

discard this standard upon accepting the theory of evolution as fact.

If fossilized evidence supports creation theory, why not embrace the current facts and the possibility of supernatural intelligence? Could it be that an entire dimension of life cannot be measured in a laboratory? Can love be analyzed in a test tube? No, but no one doubts its existence. Can we be sure that life is confined to the boundaries of human intellect? Perhaps it is profoundly unscientific to conclude that nothing exists outside of our own sphere of understanding. What if the prophets are right about the existence of another intelligence? Then the riddle of the universe is no longer shrouded in mystery.

As stated in the ancient writings, invisible energy "fueled" the birth of the cosmos according to the will of supernatural intelligence. The prophets speak of creation as an ongoing materialization of organized matter.

In contrast, existing theory speaks of an explosion of dispersing matter. Known as the "Big Bang," the theory assumes that a "cosmic egg" exploded, shooting various materials throughout the dark expanse of space. "One second, according to theory, there was nothingness. The next, our cosmos sprang into existence."[15]

Recent astronomical findings, however, have called into question this position. In the essay titled "Big Bang Theory under Fire," William C. Mitchel wrote: "[E]vidence against the BB [Big Bang] has been building to the point where the world may soon start to doubt it."[16]

Until recently, astronomers had generally believed that the cosmic expansion was gradually slowing down as a result of the gravitational attraction exerted within the known universe. This logic was not lost on the Big Bang theory, which assumed that a cosmic blast would ultimately produce a decelerating cosmic expansion, the obvious assumption being that an explosion that took place billions of years ago would be slowing down by now.

The problem with this assumption is that the cosmos is engaged in the opposite direction. Astronomers have discovered "that some mysterious force . . . [is] acting against the pull of gravity, causing galaxies to fly away from each other at ever greater speeds. . . . In one sense, the idea is not completely new. Einstein had included such an 'anti-gravity' effect in his theory of general relativity."[17] Yet, as the twentieth century drew to a close, "no one expected that the effect would turn out to be real."[18] Recent astronomical findings reveal that invisible energy is driving the galactic expansion "and it seems likely now that this expansion will continue indefinitely."[19]

This finding has given birth to a new theory called the "Big Rip." It is a "harrowing new theory about the death of the universe [which] paints a picture of 'phantom energy' ripping apart galaxies, stars, planets and eventually every speck of matter in a fantastical end to time."[20] Robert Caldwell of Dartmouth University—lead author of this theory—explains that it is one possible outcome for solid astronomical observations made in the late 1990s. (It wasn't long ago that many cosmologists believed the universe might reverse course, and that normal gravity would win, causing everything to collapse back on itself in a "Big Crunch.")

The energy that is driving the "Big Rip" is now referred to as "dark energy." What is dark energy? At this time, scientists cannot explain it; they can only detect it.

Adding to this cosmic puzzle, astronomers have discovered the presence of unseen matter in space. Called "dark matter," this material represents another unseen force in the cosmos, and some forms of this material are theorized to be radically different from matter found on Earth.

Ordinary matter on this planet is composed of protons, neutrons, and electrons, otherwise known collectively as atoms. Although the newly discovered dark matter exhibits this type of structure, more exotic forms of this material are thought to be composed of a "sea of massive particles."[21]

The discovery of dark matter is considered to be "groundbreaking." This unseen matter exerts a gravitational pull on celestial objects, and "by measuring these mysterious effects of gravity, researchers determine how much 'extra' gravity is present, and hence how much extra mass, or dark matter, must exist."[22]

Kim Griest, a physicist at the University of California, has worked since the mid-1990s on a project called "microlensing." It is a process used to "infer the presence of unseen objects by noting how more distant light is bent as it travels past the hidden object."[23] With this system came the discovery of dark matter.

> More than three dozen elusive white dwarf stars have been found in a halo of objects surrounding our galaxy, marking the first direct evidence for previously unseen "dark matter" and lending support to a widely held theory that there is much more to the universe than meets the eye.[24] . . . "[C]urrent theories can't cope" with such a finding and it would "trigger a revolution" in ideas about how galaxies and stars form and evolve.[25]

The coming revolution in thinking regarding the origin of the universe and its continuing expansion is the direct result of unseen forces at work in the cosmos. Traditional theories find no comfort in this new astronomical evidence. Could it be that the cosmic expansion is not slowing down because there never was an explosion to begin with?

As William Mitchel reminded all of us: "It is all but forgotten that the BB [Big Bang] is not fact, but an unproven theory."[26] Not only is it unproven, the theory has already gone bust in the minds of many scientific thinkers. As cited by Eric J. Lerner in his book, *The Big Bang Never Happened*: "[I]n the past few years, observation after observation has contradicted the predictions of this theory."[27]

Recent astronomical findings are overturning traditional thinking regarding the cosmos and, simultaneously, the collected data point to huge gaps in our understanding. As stated by astronomer Richard Ellis of Caltech: "I find it very worrying that you

Creation: Theory and Prophecy 39

have a universe where there are three constituents, of which only one [i.e., ordinary matter] is really physically understood."[28]

If astronomers acknowledge the presence of energy and matter that exceeds our current understanding, then what else in the cosmos exceeds our understanding? If life exists among ordinary visible matter, does life exist among invisible matter? Why couldn't there be unseen intelligence that exists in another world, in another life-form? Can spirit beings and angels also exist?

If unseen forces are at work throughout the galaxies, are unseen forces also at work upon the Earth? Could it be that recent astronomical evidence is just beginning to reveal the fingerprints of a higher intelligence?

If science has provided a new understanding of the cosmos, it cannot help but alter the way we think about the origin of the universe, man, and his destiny. Truly, there is more to the universe than can be detected by normal, empirical means. If our long-held assumptions about creation are incorrect, then where is the human mind to turn?

At the start of the twenty-first century, we should ask: Is it more logical to conclude that the prophets were divinely inspired? Or were they just trying to explain our world with their own understanding of it? It cannot be both: the ancient writings either speak of our past and future or they do not. Unquestionably, logic exists to support their validity.

Pursuing this thought (of existing logic), I would like to turn your attention to the archaeological community—as it pertains to the Middle East. In the mid-nineteenth century, archaeological explorers were drawn to the Holy Land in search of the past. Their collective efforts focused on one central thought: to determine the accuracy of history chronicled in the Bible. After 150+ years of searching, the results obtained by the archaeological community have been staggering. David Rohl, author of *A Test of Time* states: "Without initially starting out to discover the historical Bible, I have come to the

Creation: Theory and Prophecy 41

conclusion that much of the Old Testament contains real history."[29]

In essence, archaeologists have discovered corroborating evidence from extrabiblical sources, and on numerous occasions have demonstrated the reliability and plausibility of what was recorded thousands of years ago. Through ancient artifacts, scientists have given the modern world a glimpse into life that once was, revealing a voice that speaks to us from the past.[30]

With regard to the authenticity of the biblical texts, extraordinary evidence surfaced in the mid-twentieth century. The Dead Sea Scrolls, which have been referred to by scholars as the greatest manuscript discovery of modern times, were discovered between 1947 and 1956 in caves along the shore of the Dead Sea. Among the 800+ scrolls are the oldest known versions of all but one of the books of the Old Testament. The rest offer an intriguing picture of life in the Holy Land at the time Jesus taught in Jerusalem.

The conclusion drawn by scholars is that the biblical texts found in the scrolls are in substantial agreement with translations of the Old Testament used today. Significant among the scrolls is a virtually intact copy of Isaiah; it predates the earliest known Isaiah manuscript by 1,000 years.

Scientists have concluded that the Dead Sea Scrolls were transcribed between the years 200 B.C. and A.D. 68. (This conclusion is based on carbon 14 dating: a highly accurate process that measures the decay of carbon 14—a radioactive element that erodes at a constant rate over time.) Of additional importance, the scientific community revealed that the critical biblical manuscripts were dated prior to 100 B.C. This is dramatic because the biblical scrolls found in the twentieth century provided documentation that the Messianic prophecies (about the first coming of Christ) were written before the dawn of the first century.

The prophets who wrote to us *during* the first century—speaking about the fulfillment of these Messianic prophecies—revealed that another world of invisible, Spirit life, communicated divine prophecy to Earth by way of the man called Jesus. The prophecy spoken in the first century declared that Jesus of Nazareth was the living word of supernatural intelligence—in the flesh. If such a person did exist, he would be the prophet of all prophets.

The record that Jesus lived in the Holy Land is not disputed. Reputable historians agree that the story of this "prophet" was not just a legend; historical writings support the claims made about him. Hence, it is not a matter of whether Jesus lived, but rather, was he the Son of God?

Some people dismiss Jesus Christ as a fake hero. Yet millions hail him as Savior and Lord. Whatever people think of him, nobody can deny that his life represented a pivotal point in human history. His influence on humanity is unquestioned. No other great leader has inspired so many people, in so many countries, over the course of so much time.

Historian Philip Schaff described the overwhelming influence of Christ's life:

> This Jesus of Nazareth, without money and arms, conquered more millions than Alexander, Caesar . . . and Napoleon; without science . . . he shed more light on things human and divine than all philosophers and scholars combined; without the eloquence of schools, he spoke such words of life as were never spoken before or since, and produced effects which lie beyond the reach of orator or poet; without writing a single line, he set more pens in motion, and furnished themes for more sermons, orations, discussions, learned volumes, works of art, and songs of praise than the whole army of great men of ancient and modern times.[31]

By the time Jesus taught in Jerusalem, over one thousand years' worth of written prophecy had already gone before him. Beginning with Moses, every prophet recorded some-

Creation: Theory and Prophecy 45

thing about the coming Messiah, the Christ, and nearly two thousand years ago, a man named Jesus declared that he was the Son of God. Additionally, the words he spoke were revolutionary.

He said that human souls will cross the spiritual divide and shall live in spiritual bodies in a new world. Christ painted the bridge that spans the chasm between the two points in time. He revealed the hereafter and empowered man to arrive there. These visions—given by Jesus and recorded by the prophets—give a clear view of what is yet to be.

Irrefutable scientific evidence has given us reason to believe that divine prophecy is not simply the product of fertile and imaginative minds. If this were the case, then it is not a matter of whether Earth has been informed of its future but a matter of whether its population heeds it.

Astronomers and archeologists have given us an entirely new way of looking at the Earth and the cosmos. Perhaps we all owe it to ourselves to be open to another way of knowing.

Act One

1

SPIRITUAL WARFARE

Destiny is not a matter of chance, it is a matter of choice; it is not a thing to be waited for, it is a thing to be achieved.

—William Jennings Bryan

Introduction

The history of mankind identifies a fascination with prophecies and life in the hereafter. As intelligent life we have a conscious awareness of our past and present, but do we have a future that extends beyond death? No question on Earth has received more attention. Whether embracing life after death, or accepting no exit from this world, the question remains central to all philosophies and religions. Even if one dismisses the existence of life on the other side, the question of one's real purpose in this life requires an answer. Ironically, an honest pursuit to find one's destiny invariably leads straight back to a familiar thought: Why are we here in the first place?

The answer is divided along two lines: either there is a divine purpose for the Earth or there isn't. We are simply passing through history, or history is being made through us—in the form of a greater, supernatural purpose.

Fundamentally, we all seek the obvious: love, belonging, and a sense of worth that satisfies the soul. Whether we are a success or a failure in these vital areas of life is determined by our beliefs. What we believe determines what we become. Our response as intelligent human beings should be only to take great care in determining our personal convictions.

Unfortunately, the history of man has demonstrated that beliefs—be they personal or societal—are too often based on speculation and false information and not on scientific fact, or an underlying, inherent truth. In the seventeenth century the famous astronomer Galileo said that Earth revolved around the sun and was arrested for it. In essence, that moment in time represented the struggle that has saturated recorded history—the forces that seek enlightenment and the forces that seek to extinguish it.

As we look around at this creation on Earth, there is plenty that is good and plenty that is evil. One response could be to focus on the disorder of the world, and conclude that humankind simply evolved—believing that there is no divine design behind creation. In modern times, we find that this conclusion has saturated the human psyche. I submit to you that this is precisely what the enemy of God (called Satan) wants mankind to believe. Why? The soul. There is a battle for your soul, and the war is waged with words.

For the moment, allow yourself the opportunity to explore this thought. What if you do have a soul? What if there is a Creator who designed the human body to live on the Earth and built into it a soul? If this is the case, then it stands to reason that our response would be to understand the importance of the soul, and the purpose of our existence on this planet. It also stands to reason that the Creator would communicate the answers to these questions (the truth) in a fashion that could be understood.

Clearly, truth and deception live side by side in the world. I submit to you that one spiritual power (who is behind the disorder of this world) seeks for you to be *deceived* (thereby *destroying* the soul), and the other spiritual power (who created the order of this world) seeks for you to be *enlightened* (thereby *liberating* the soul).

Spiritual Warfare

We can ill afford to allow spiritual deception to be woven into the fabric of our thinking patterns. The purifying of thought—through immutable knowledge acquired—cannot help but yield an enhanced personal reality.

With these thoughts in mind, we shall now embark on a journey that goes to the very core of this battle for the soul—to the very core of human existence.

Setting the Stage

> [W]e speak of God's secret wisdom, a wisdom that has been hidden and that God destined for our glory before time began. None of the rulers of this age understood it, for if they had, they would not have crucified the Lord of glory.
>
> —The Apostle Paul (1 Cor. 2:7, 8)

In the beginning, when God stretched forth the cosmos, evil was unknown. The Creator purposed that within his divine creation would reside two types of beings: angelic and human. Spirit beings would inhabit the heavens, and human beings would inhabit the Earth.

When the Creator brought forth Lucifer, that angel entered the heavenly realm as an eternal spirit. God anointed him as "guardian cherub," bestowing upon him the honor and authority to accomplish his (God's) will.

In the Garden of Eden, God directed energy upon the elements of this planet and brought forth another type of creation: flesh and blood. The soul of God was manifested on Earth when he breathed the breath of life into Adam. Humankind would reflect its Creator in the physical realm, just as Lucifer had in the spiritual realm.

God—the eternal King—is holy and righteous, and that's how he created his creation. Free will, given by God, would enable the Father to coexist with his independent "intelligence." With that free will, however, came active rebellion against the eternal King, resulting in a loss of harmony within both the heavenly and the earthly realms.

Whereas Lucifer sought to usurp the throne of God, Adam and Eve succumbed to deception in Eden. Unholy created beings then existed within creation, and spiritual warfare raged against the Creator. Lucifer's expressed intent was to displace God and ascend to his throne.

However, the guardian cherub overestimated the value of his initiative. The progress of dark spiritual power would be reversed by way of flesh and blood; it would come in the form of God's only begotten Son, Jesus Christ. The eternal King purposed that through the planned death of Jesus, souls upon Earth could be liberated from mortality.

The fallen angel never would have crucified the Messiah had he known the consequences.

The Ancient Writings

Lucifer literally means "morning star," and it is the name that God gave to his angelic "model of perfection." Created as a magnificent angel, Lucifer was with God on the holy mount, the pinnacle of Heaven. The guardian cherub walked faultlessly in all of his ways until evil was conceived within. Lucifer became obsessed with what was reserved for God: worship. Therewith, the angel of light turned to darkness:

> You [Lucifer] were the model of perfection, full of wisdom and perfect in beauty. You were in Eden, the garden of God; every precious stone adorned you. . . . You were anointed as a guardian cherub, for so I ordained you. You were on the holy mount of God; you walked among the fiery stones. You were blameless in your ways from the day you were created till wickedness was found in you. . . . So I drove you in disgrace from the mount of God, and I expelled you, O guardian cherub, from among the fiery stones. Your heart became proud on account of your beauty, and you corrupted your wisdom because of your splendor. (Ezek. 28:12–17)

> How you have fallen from heaven,
> O morning star, son of the dawn! . . .
> You said in your heart, "I will ascend to
> heaven; I will raise my throne above the
> stars of God; I will sit enthroned on the
> mount of assembly, on the utmost
> heights of the sacred mountain. I will
> ascend above the tops of the clouds; I
> will make myself like the Most High."
> (Isa. 14:12–14)

The former guardian cherub spoke his prophecy into the ears of Heaven: the throne of Heaven would be his. He would be like the Most High.

By his own power, Lucifer transformed himself into the highest-ranking dark angel: Satan. Immediately, the son of the dawn became the angel of darkness. Pride extinguished divine light, and wisdom was corrupted. Now, the fallen angel would rule his *own* kingdom, having ultimate command over one-third of the angels (those who chose to reject Heaven with Lucifer).

With his spiritual power, Satan would use Earth as the means to gain the "utmost heights of the sacred mountain." By tempting mankind to commit treason against God, the fallen angel would divide Heaven and Earth. Sin would cause the soul life of man to die and that would separate the immortal God from his mortal creation. The fallen angel would cause this calamity by initiating a rebellion upon Earth by deception.

Satan knew the prophecy that God had given in the Garden of Eden, that Adam and Eve did not have the right to distort the standard of truth regarding good and evil. Satan would claim the opposite; the fallen angel would give man the false sense of security that he could be as a god. But the true God had already told Adam that he would surely die if he ate of that "fruit":

> [T]he Lord God commanded the man, "You are free to eat from any tree in the garden; but you must not eat from the tree of the knowledge of good and evil, for when you eat of it you will surely die." (Gen. 2:16, 17)

By man's eating the fruit, human creation would no longer be in harmony with the Creator. Partaking of the tree would be much more than innocent self-interest; it would be an act of defiance, and by doing so, Adam and Eve would determine for themselves what is "good" and what is "evil." The one-time guardian cherub became fixated on bringing this to pass.

On the day that Satan appeared as an angel of light, he spoke beautifully about the deadly tree.

> Now the serpent was more crafty than any of the wild animals the Lord God had made. He said to the woman, "Did God really say, 'You must not eat from any tree in the garden'?"
>
> The woman said to the serpent, "We may eat fruit from the trees in the garden, but God did say, 'You must not eat fruit from the tree that is in the middle of the garden, and you must not touch it, or you will die.'"

> "You will not surely die," the serpent said to the woman. "For God knows that when you eat of it your eyes will be opened, and you will be like God, knowing good and evil."
>
> When the woman saw that the fruit of the tree was good for food and pleasing to the eye, and also desirable for gaining wisdom, she took some and ate it. She also gave some to her husband, who was with her, and he ate it. Then the eyes of both of them were opened, and they realized they were naked; so they sewed fig leaves together and made coverings for themselves. (Gen. 3:1–7)

In desiring to be as God, Adam and Eve broke from God. Once their eyes were opened to this fact, the two realized that they were no longer covered by God's righteousness. Humankind now saw their flesh and blood as sinful.

In Eden, Satan accused God of deliberately denying Adam and Eve from attaining an advanced state. He claimed that God was keeping them from becoming gods. Eve believed Satan; therefore, Eve ascribed evil to God. She called him a liar, just as Satan had.

Ironically, Satan was correct about the eyes of man being opened, but instead of becoming gods, Adam and Eve realized their reduced stature in creation. The prophecy from God was true and the ramifications were soon to follow.

> Then the man and his wife heard the sound of the Lord God as he was walking in the garden in the cool of the day, and they hid from the Lord God among the trees of the garden. But the Lord God called to the man, "Where are you?"
>
> He answered, "I heard you in the garden, and I was afraid because I was naked; so I hid."
>
> And he said, "Who told you that you were naked? Have you eaten from the tree that I commanded you not to eat from?"
>
> The man said, "The woman you put here with me—she gave me some fruit from the tree, and I ate it."

> Then the Lord God said to the woman, "What is this you have done?"
>
> The woman said, "The serpent deceived me, and I ate." (Gen. 3:8–13)

Righteousness was lost in Eden. Therefore, Adam feared God and hid from him. As sin had caused a separation between man and his Creator, paradise would now come to an abrupt halt.

Masquerading as an angel of light, Satan had beguiled man into desiring what he himself had succumbed to: the desire to be as God. With this act, humankind could no longer have access to the tree of life.

> And the Lord God said, "The man has now become like one of us, knowing good and evil. He must not be allowed to reach out his hand and take also from the tree of life and eat, and live forever."
>
> So the Lord God banished him from the Garden of Eden to work the ground from which he had been taken. (Gen. 3:22, 23)

Now denied access to the tree, unholy man was separated from the divine. In a moment of time, the human soul became mortal. The Creator could not allow sinful man to live forever in Eden because that would have yielded permanent disharmony in creation.

Despite the separation, God promised that he would reverse the consequences facing the offspring of Adam and Eve. He prophesied that a Savior would be sent to release man from the slavery of mortality. Simultaneously, the Lord God condemned Satan for his treachery:

> So the Lord God said to the serpent, "Because you have done this, Cursed are you above all the livestock and all the wild animals! You will crawl on your belly and you will eat dust all the days of your life. And I will put enmity between you and the woman [Eve], and between your offspring and hers; he [Christ] will crush your head." (Gen. 3:14, 15)

The prophecy from God was that his Son would crush the hope of darkness. Never would the fallen angel recover from the wound that Christ would inflict.

What Lucifer had initiated, God would finish.

> "Now will I arise," says the Lord. "Now will I be exalted; now will I be lifted up." (Isa. 33:10)

> I [will] bring forth a fire from the midst of thee, it shall devour thee, and I will bring thee to ashes upon the earth in the sight of all them that behold thee . . . and never *shalt* thou *be* any more. (Ezek. 28:18, 19 KJV)

God decreed Satan's fate: ashes. Yet the fallen angel intended to defeat this prophecy; he would refute Heaven by crucifying the Christ.

The fallen angel would bring an end to Jesus through the religious leaders in Jerusalem known as the Pharisees and

Sadducees. These counterfeit temple authorities would participate in the conspiracy to kill Jesus of Nazareth, for his life threatened their very existence.

> Then the chief priests and the Pharisees called a meeting of the Sanhedrin [high court]. "What are we accomplishing?" they asked. "Here is this man [Jesus] performing many miraculous signs. If we let him go on like this, everyone will believe in him, and then the Romans will come and take away both our place and our nation."
>
> Then one of them, named Caiaphas, who was high priest that year, spoke up, "You know nothing at all! You do not realize that it is better for you that one man die for the people than that the whole nation perish."
>
> He did not say this on his own, but as high priest that year he prophesied that Jesus would die for the Jewish nation. . . . So from that day on they plotted to take his life. (John 11:47–51, 53)

The temple authorities were concerned about their "place" in Israel and potentially losing the entire country to the Romans. Jesus *had* to die if both were to be saved. Hence, the fulfillment of Satan's purpose would come by way of flesh and blood.

This conflict in Jerusalem was the flash point between two spiritual powers. Whereas evil manifested itself through the Pharisees and Sadducees, the divine power of Heaven manifested itself through the Son of God. In Christ's verbal exchange with his adversaries, he disclosed their hypocrisy and identified their true nature.

> As it is, you are determined to kill me, a man who has told you the truth that I heard from God. . . . You are doing the things your own father does. . . . If God were your Father, you would love me, for I came from God and now am here. I have not come on my own; but he sent me. . . . You belong to your father, the devil, and you want to carry out your father's desire. He was a mur-

derer from the beginning, not holding to the truth, for there is no truth in him. When he lies, he speaks his native language, for he is a liar and the father of lies. (John 8:40–42, 44)

The fallen angel had darkened the minds of those who sat upon the seat of religious authority. Their souls belonged to darkness—sealed shut by the seed of Satan.

The Sanhedrin's perception of reality demanded the death of Earth's Messiah. Therein, the children of darkness would fulfill the will of their father; they would falsely accuse Jesus of blasphemy against God to carry out their own agenda.

> The high priest said to him, "I charge you under oath by the living God: Tell us if you are the Christ, the Son of God."
>
> "Yes, it is as you say," Jesus replied. "But I say to all of you: In the future you will see the Son of Man sitting at the right hand of the Mighty One and coming on the clouds of heaven."

> Then the high priest tore his clothes and said, "He has spoken blasphemy! Why do we need any more witnesses? Look, now you have heard the blasphemy. What do you think?"
>
> "He is worthy of death," they answered. (Matt. 26:63–66)

Accused of lying, Jesus would face crucifixion. Therein, the dark angel believed that he would stop the kingdom of God through Jesus' death—blotting out the light sent by Heaven.

In reality, the fallen angel participated in giving mankind the ultimate sacrifice for sin—the children of darkness slew God's Lamb: "Christ, our Passover lamb, has been sacrificed" (1 Cor. 5:7). Just as the Passover lamb in Egypt saved Israelites from death, so the Lamb of God would save souls from mortality. Jesus sacrificed his own life so that others could live eternally. With his Resurrection, he offered himself to the Father in Heaven as the ultimate atonement for sin.

> For Christ did not enter a man-made sanctuary that was only a copy of the true one; he entered heaven itself, now to appear for us in God's presence. . . . [H]e has appeared once for all at the end of the ages to do away with sin by the sacrifice of himself. (Heb. 9:24, 26)

Jesus' sacrifice did "away with sin" and its consequences. He did not receive the sinful nature that Adam had passed on to humankind because God was his Father; therefore, he was in a position to live a sinless life and die as God's gift to Earth. Hence, any person who accepts this sacrifice is granted eternal life.

Satan lost his trump card over man because mortality of the soul was permanently affected. Christ "destroyed" the dark angel by nullifying his power over death: "[B]y his [Jesus'] death he might destroy him who holds the power of death—that is, the devil—and free those who all their lives were held in slavery by their fear of death" (Heb. 2:14, 15).

Freedom from the fear of death is central to Christ's gospel of immortality. This became a reality by way of the Crucifixion and Resurrection. Eternal life for human souls was not what Satan had envisioned when Jesus bled on the Cross. Preoccupied with Jesus' death, the fallen angel could not foresee the ramifications of his actions.

The dark angel not only lost his power over death but also lost his position in the heavenly realm. For, after Christ ascended to his throne, the archangel Michael waged war against Satan.

> And there was war in heaven. Michael and his angels fought against the dragon, and the dragon and his angels fought back. But he was not strong enough, and they lost their place in heaven. The great dragon was hurled down—that ancient serpent called the devil, or Satan, who leads the whole world astray. He was hurled to the earth, and his angels with him. (Rev. 12:7–9)[1]

Unable to withstand the power of the enthroned Christ and the strength of the angels, Satan was driven from his perch. First cast from the pinnacle of Heaven by God, Satan would now no longer have access to the heavenly realm itself. The fallen angel was now confined to an earthly realm that would one day be the scene of his final undoing.

With the dark angel removed, humankind no longer had an accuser in the presence of God (Job 1), but an advocate. The Son of God displaced the one-time guardian cherub and became man's intercessor. Christ was placed in a position to release souls from death and grant eternal life for all who overcome deception and reach to the heavens through him.

> Therefore he is able to save completely those who come to God through him, because he always lives to intercede for them. . . . We do have such a high priest, who sat down at the right hand of the throne of the Majesty in heaven, and who serves in the sanctuary, the true

> tabernacle set up by the Lord, not by man. (Heb. 7:25; 8:1, 2)

Situated in the true tabernacle in Heaven, man's great high priest was positioned to intercede in the lives of souls upon Earth. Through the Messiah, man would finally be empowered to exit the death sentence passed on from Adam.

> Therefore, just as sin entered the world through one man [Adam], and death through sin, and in this way death came to all men . . . For if the many died by the trespass of the one man, how much more did God's grace and the gift that came by the grace of the one man, Jesus Christ, overflow to the many! (Rom. 5:12, 15)

> For since death came through a man, the resurrection of the dead comes also through a man. For as in Adam all die, so in Christ all will be made alive. But each in his own turn: Christ, the first-

fruits; then, when he comes, those who belong to him. (1 Cor. 15:21–23)

Christ was the "firstfruits" from the dead, and those who "belong to him" shall also be "made alive" (immortal) when he returns from Heaven.

Ultimately, the destiny of all souls lies with God or Satan. Earthly inhabitants have free will to embrace divine light or reject it. A person forfeits the game, becoming a soul lost forever, when darkness is accepted.

The fallen angel wields the power of death by inducing the false pleasure of rejecting God. Satan lures his prey away from the truth and into a life void of meaning. Thereby, darkened minds feed upon thoughts of spiritual deception. Empty words are served by the voice of demonic power; all the lies that discredit the light of Heaven pour forth to twist human logic. The foundational fallacy promoted by Satan is that mankind can gain some greater reward on this Earth. However, as Christ proclaimed: "What good is it for a man to gain the whole world, yet forfeit his soul?" (Mark 8:36).

The lie is to live in this world as if there is nothing to lose. The question asked by the Son of God was to weigh the alternative. According to Christ, there is something to lose—the soul.

The soul is the life that springs from the seed passed on from Adam. "For the [soul] life of the flesh *is* in the blood [the life-giving source within humankind]" (Lev. 17:11 KJV).

In humankind, there exists a distinction between souls. If the soul is not forfeited, it will live on the other side. In contrast, if the soul is "ruined," it can never regenerate itself. That is why Christ forewarned the world of Satan's power: "Do not be afraid of those who kill the body but cannot kill the soul. Rather, be afraid of the One [Satan] who can destroy [ruin] both soul and body in hell" (Matt. 10:28). "Hell," spoken here by Jesus, is the future funeral pyre—the "devouring judgment fire" (*Gehenna* in the Greek language).

Satan, who is the god of this age, destroys the mind, and thereby the soul, by a web of lies, for his distortion causes unbelief: "The god of this age has blinded the minds of unbelievers, so that they cannot see the light of the gospel of the glory of Christ, who is the image of God" (2 Cor. 4:4). Those who are blinded by Satan cannot see the darkness that pulses in the airwaves of life because they are in the midst of it. Without words of light, the eyes are blind and the soul is held captive.

God's response to Earth is to embrace his Son, "[who is] a light for the Gentiles, [sent] to open eyes that are blind, to free captives from prison and to release from the dungeon those who sit in darkness" (Isa. 42:6, 7). When the door is opened to Christ, liberation from darkness follows. The spiritual light of Christ exposes the web of lies crafted by forces that oppose Heaven.

There *is* another dimension to this physical world. The matrix of spiritual energy that encompasses the globe is seen through spiritual eyes. When divine light fills the soul, it awakens the mind to a new level of perception. Without it, the spiritual dimension upon Earth remains misunderstood: "The man without the Spirit does not accept the things that come from the Spirit of God, for they are foolishness to him, and he cannot understand them, because they are spiritually discerned" (1 Cor. 2:14).

To "discern" is to perceive by sight or other means. In this case, it means to perceive life from a spiritual perspective. It is to understand the will of Heaven in this world.

God's will is that no soul die a death from which there is no escape. This is divine prophecy spoken by the Lord God: "As surely as I live, declares the Sovereign Lord, I take no pleasure in the death of the wicked, but rather that they turn from their ways and live" (Ezek. 33:11).

In the Holy Land, Jesus said, "[Y]ou will know the truth, and the truth will set you free" (John 8:32). Freedom means no longer being a slave to sin and its consequences. In the spiritual war fought upon Earth, truth is the key to alter the fate of the soul: "Whoever turns a sinner from the error of his way will save him [his soul] from death and cover over a multitude of sins" (James 5:20).

Death of the soul is permanently dealt with by the conversion of the soul from darkness to light. Sins are forever "hidden" from the Father, and guilt is removed. Therein, Christ's destruction of Lucifer's power becomes a personal reality: "[T]he one who is in you [Christ] is greater than the one who is in the world [Satan]" (1 John 4:4). A soul that is saved from death is secured from the power of darkness, and takes on a spiritual nature that is sealed by Heaven.

The Almighty God did not bring forth this creation in vain. With it, the Father will fulfill his plan to live with his sons without the presence of darkness. The invisible Creator has fully disclosed his strategy in written form, and Satan is powerless to alter the future. The battle plans are already drawn, and the outcome is without doubt: souls will be saved from death because the Messiah won the right to ransom them from the power of the grave. In this spiritual conflict for the soul, the eternal King claims victory when Satan loses a human soul to eternity.

2

EVENTS OF THE END: THE SEVEN SEALS OF CHRIST'S PROPHECY

[T]he sun will be darkened, and the moon will not give its light; the stars will fall from the sky, and the heavenly bodies will be shaken. At that time men will see the Son of Man coming in clouds with great power and glory. And he will send his angels and gather his elect from the four winds, from the ends of the earth to the ends of the heavens.[1]

—The Son of God (Mark 13:24–27)

At the end of the first century, the Son of God descended from Heaven and appeared in his glorified form to the apostle John. It was during this appearance that Christ revealed the chronological sequence of end-time events, providing a virtual motion picture of the drama that shall unfold on Earth and what waits in the hereafter.

In a vision, John would see the "Ark of the Covenant"—the Word of God itself. Found in the sanctuary of Heaven, it represents God's commitment to all mankind, that prophecies found in the prophetic texts are not void of power. This Ark had been opened by divine will, and Christ would make known its contents to John. With this divine revelation, John would write the last book of the Bible: the Book of Revelation.

John opened his book by recording the appearance of the glorified Christ, describing him as human-like in organization but entirely spiritual in nature. Not only did the apostle see his Lord but he also witnessed first hand the spiritual body that awaits those who shall live on the other side.

> On the Lord's Day I [John] was in the Spirit, and I heard behind me a loud voice like a trumpet. . . . I turned around to see the voice that was speaking to me. And when I turned I saw . . . someone "like a son of man," dressed in a robe reaching down to his feet and with a golden sash around his chest. His head and hair were white like wool, as white as snow, and his eyes were like blazing fire. His feet were like bronze glowing in a furnace, and his voice was like the sound of rushing waters. . . . His face was like the sun shining in all its brilliance. When I saw him, I fell at his feet as though dead. Then he placed his right hand on me and said: "Do not be afraid. I am the First and the Last. I am the Living One; I was dead, and behold I am alive for ever and ever!" (Rev. 1:10, 12–18)

The once-crucified Messiah now stood before his apostle to impart divine revelation (spiritual energy) by way of visions. The presentation began after John stepped through a door in his mind to Heaven.

> After this I [John] looked, and there before me was a door standing open in heaven. And the voice I had first heard speaking to me like a trumpet said, "Come up here, and I will show you what must take place after this." At once I was in the Spirit, and there before me was a throne in heaven with someone sitting on it. And the one who sat there had the appearance of jasper and carnelian [precious stones]. A rainbow, resembling an emerald, encircled the throne. . . . Then I saw in the right hand of him who sat on the throne a scroll with writing on both sides and sealed with seven seals. (Rev. 4:1–3; 5:1)

John saw the seat of Heaven's authority—the throne of the eternal King. The supreme

Creator appeared as precious gems, and a spectrum of light formed a halo that adorned the throne.

In the vision, John saw in the hand of the King a scroll "sealed with seven seals." As this scroll opened, so was John's mind opened to divine intervention. With each seal, John saw moving pictures that reached deeper and deeper into the future.

The apocalyptic scene began after the first four seals opened, and the eternal King released his horsemen. What John saw was the "Four Horsemen of the Apocalypse" loosed upon Earth to fulfill Heaven's will.

> I [John] watched as the Lamb [Christ] opened the first of the seven seals. Then I heard one of the four living creatures say in a voice like thunder, "Come!" I looked, and there before me was a white horse! Its rider held a bow, and he was given a crown, and he rode out as a conqueror bent on conquest. When the Lamb opened the second seal, I heard the second living creature say,

"Come!" Then another horse came out, a fiery red one. Its rider was given power to take peace from the earth and to make men slay each other. To him was given a large sword. When the Lamb opened the third seal, I heard the third living creature say, "Come!" I looked, and there before me was a black horse! Its rider was holding a pair of scales in his hand. . . . When the Lamb opened the fourth seal, I heard the voice of the fourth living creature say, "Come!" I looked, and there before me was a pale horse! Its rider was named Death, and Hades [the grave] was following close behind him. They were given power over a fourth of the earth to kill by sword, famine and plague, and by the wild beasts of the earth. (Rev. 6:1–5, 7, 8)

These are the four spirits of heaven, going out from standing in the presence of the Lord of the whole world. (Zech. 6:5)

Events of the End:
The Seven Seals of Christ's Prophecy

The four horsemen shall prepare Earth for the most dramatic event modern man has ever witnessed: the second coming of Jesus Christ (which shall occur after the sixth seal opens).

Invisible to the human eye, the four horsemen will have a spiritual and physical impact on flesh and blood. Whereas the angel upon the white horse brings God's righteousness to conquer spiritual darkness, the red horse brings war. Whereas the black horse brings God's spiritual judgment, the pale rider brings its physical consequence: death.

These angelic forces that proceed from the eternal throne shall bring Heaven's justice to the planet. Injustice found on Earth shall be met with overwhelming consequences. These earthly consequences are the "birth pains" that the world shall endure until the time of the sixth seal, when the Earth gives "birth" to the righteous souls that shall ascend off the planet.

With the King's horsemen upon Earth, only one seal will separate the population from the return of Christ: the fifth. It represents the last "invisible" mark on the heavenly clock. It is the final unseen sign. The fifth seal shall yield another dramatic spiritual event: souls shall rise from the grave, clothed in spiritual bodies.

> When he opened the fifth seal, I saw under the altar the souls of those who had been slain because of the word of God and the testimony they had maintained. They called out in a loud voice, "How long, Sovereign Lord, holy and true, until you judge the inhabitants of the earth and avenge our blood?" Then each of them was given a white robe, and they were told to wait a little longer, until the number of their fellow servants and brothers who were to be killed as they had been was completed. (Rev. 6:9–11)

When the martyrs are released to Heaven, their souls shall be clothed in the spiritual light of Heaven's righteousness. This seal

Events of the End:
The Seven Seals of Christ's Prophecy

brings not only an awakening to eternal life, but also a cry for justice. The assurance given by Heaven is that the martyrs need only "wait a little longer" for the judgment they seek because justice shall be delivered after the seventh seal opens.

With the resurrected martyrs in Heaven and the four horsemen fulfilling their charge on Earth, the stage is then set for the return of God's Son, and, unlike the first five seals, when the sixth seal is loosed, it will shock the population. The sixth seal not only marks the second coming of Christ but also announces the coming wrath.

> I watched as he opened the sixth seal. There was a great earthquake. The sun turned black . . . the whole moon turned blood red, and the stars in the sky fell to earth. . . . The sky receded like a scroll, rolling up, and every mountain and island was removed from its place. Then the kings of the earth, the princes, the generals, the rich, the

> mighty, and every slave and every free man hid in caves and among the rocks of the mountains. They called to the mountains and the rocks, "Fall on us and hide us from the face of him who sits on the throne and from the wrath of the Lamb! For the great day of their wrath has come, and who can stand?" (Rev. 6:12–17)

When darkness surrounds the planet, stars shoot upon the horizon, celestial bodies shift out of place, and the moon turns blood red, the deceptive calm upon Earth shall end abruptly. With this colossal presentation, Heaven shall put the nations on notice that a threshold has been reached: divine intervention shall rescue those who pursued righteousness, and divine judgment shall be upon those who rejected it. In the midst of global darkness, when the nations upon Earth mourn, crying out, "hide us from the face of him who sits on the throne," the saved of Earth shall exit the doomed planet and meet the Lord in the air.

When the sixth seal opens, the Lord Jesus Christ will return with his angels to gather God's possessions, and the sky will be filled with souls marked by Heaven. Then the sky will recede upward like a scroll, and the immortal souls shall ascend to Heaven with the angels. The remaining population will erupt into chaos, seeking to be hidden from the God whom they rejected.

The Son of God issued this dual prophecy to John, just as he had decades earlier, when he first taught in the Holy Land.

> There will be signs in the sun, moon and stars. On the earth, nations will be in anguish and perplexity at the roaring and tossing of the sea. Men will faint from terror, apprehensive of what is coming on the world, for the heavenly bodies will be shaken. At that time they will see the Son of Man coming in a cloud with power and great glory. When these things begin to take place, stand up and lift up your heads, because your redemption is drawing near. (Luke 21:25–28)

Jesus foretold that the Redemption of souls—purchased by his blood—would occur following an overwhelming celestial presentation. Years later, Christ gave revelation to both John and Paul regarding the details of this monumental future event.

John foresaw that the entire population would be locked in a stare to the heavens beholding the glorified Christ: "[H]e [Jesus] is coming with the clouds, and every eye will see him" (Rev. 1:7). That is why the rest of the world (left behind) knows "the wrath of the Lamb" is upon them. When this event finally takes place, nothing will be the same on Earth, and nothing will be the same in Heaven.

Whereas John saw the impact of the heavenly signs upon Earth's population, Paul prophesied of the impact upon the kingdom of Christ—when it is actually gathered—for to the apostle Paul, Christ revealed the glory that shall accompany his return in the sky.

> For the Lord himself will come down from heaven, with a loud com-

mand, with the voice of the archangel and with the trumpet call of God, and the dead in Christ will rise first. After that, we who are still alive and are left will be caught up together with them in the clouds to meet the Lord in the air. And so we will be with the Lord forever. (1 Thess. 4:16, 17)

With the voice of the archangel Michael, Christ shall issue a "loud command": It's time! Sleeping souls will rise from the grave made to be imperishable, and living souls shall be transformed, made to be immortal. All of them shall come together over the planet and ascend to Heaven in a supernatural form that matches the molecular structure of Christ himself. It is a structure unlike anything on Earth for it is of heavenly content:

> There are also heavenly bodies and there are earthly bodies; but the splendor of the heavenly bodies is one kind, and the splendor of the earthly bodies is another. The sun has one kind of

splendor, the moon another and the stars another; and star differs from star in splendor. So will it be with the resurrection of the dead. The body that is sown is perishable, it is raised imperishable; it is sown in dishonor, it is raised in glory; it is sown in weakness, it is raised in power; it is sown a natural body, it is raised a spiritual body. If there is a natural body, there is also a spiritual body. . . . And just as we have borne the likeness of the earthly man, so shall we bear the likeness of the man from heaven. (1 Cor. 15:40–44, 49)

Listen, I tell you a mystery: We will not all sleep, but we will all be changed—in a flash, in the twinkling of an eye, at the last trumpet. For the trumpet will sound, [and] the dead will be raised imperishable, and we [who are alive when Christ returns] will be changed. For the perishable [the dead] must clothe itself with the imperishable [everlasting life], and the mortal with immortality. When the perishable has been clothed with the imperishable, and the mortal with immortality, then the saying that is written will come true: "Death has been swallowed up in victory." "Where, O death, is your victory? Where, O death, is your sting?" (1 Cor. 15:51–55)

The power of Christ shall break the bonds of mortality and free souls for eternity. By revelation Christ said that he would take a natural body of flesh and blood and transform it into a powerful, eternal, and spiritual body, thereby defeating death forever. In a moment of time, death's power will be nullified. This is the prophecy spoken by the Lord God:

> I [God] will ransom them [the souls] from the power of the grave; I will redeem them from death. Where, O death, are your plagues? Where, O grave, is your destruction? (Hos. 13:14)

> [God] will swallow up death forever. The Sovereign Lord will wipe away

> the tears from all faces. . . . In that day they will say, "Surely this is our God; we trusted in him, and he saved us. This is the Lord, we trusted in him; let us rejoice and be glad in his salvation." (Isa. 25:8, 9)

In a vision, the apostle John saw this picture of future glory, when the redeemed of Earth stand in the presence of God, "without fault and with great joy" (Jude 24).

> I looked and there before me was a great multitude that no one could count, from every nation, tribe, people and language, standing before the throne and in front of the Lamb. They were wearing white robes and were holding palm branches in their hands. And they cried out in a loud voice:
> "Salvation belongs to our God, who sits on the throne, and to the Lamb."
> All the angels were standing around the throne and around the elders. . . . Then one of the elders asked me, "These in white robes—who are they, and where

did they come from?" I answered, "Sir, you know." And he said, "These are they who have come out of the great tribulation;[2] they have washed their robes and made them white in the blood of the Lamb. Therefore, they are before the throne of God and serve him day and night in his temple; and he who sits on the throne will spread his tent over them. Never again will they hunger; never again will they thirst. The sun will not beat upon them, nor any scorching heat. For the Lamb at the center of the throne will be their shepherd; he will lead them to springs of living water. And God will wipe away every tear from their eyes." (Rev. 7:9–11, 13–17)

This harvest of souls is the eternal kingdom gathered in the name of Jesus Christ. This innumerable multitude "washed their robes" and "made them white" in the "blood of the Lamb." The gathered souls are blameless before God, just as Christ himself is blameless.

Once in Heaven, the spiritual mysteries of eternal life shall be revealed and the rescued souls shall be immersed in the treasures of Heaven's knowledge. No longer will the mind be limited by flesh and blood; the infinite will no longer be skewed by the visible.

Yet in this transformation of understanding, human identities shall be retained. As each individual was known on Earth, so shall they be known in Heaven. As written by the apostle Paul, "then [at the second coming of Christ] I shall know fully [Heaven's knowledge], even as I am fully known [among those in Heaven]" (1 Cor. 13:12).

Once in the presence of God there shall be no tribulation or condemnation, only glory. Whereas palm branches symbolize great joy and triumph, the "shelter" is God's righteousness, covering all who are in his presence.

In sharp contrast, dread and sudden destruction shall fall upon the earthly inhabitants left behind, for the sixth seal represents instantaneous future shock delivered without prior notification:

Events of the End:
The Seven Seals of Christ's Prophecy

> [T]he day of the Lord will come like a thief in the night. While people are saying, "Peace and safety," destruction will come on them suddenly, as labor pains on a pregnant woman, and they will not escape. But you, brothers, are not in darkness so that this day should surprise you like a thief. You are all sons of the light and sons of the day. We do not belong to the night or to the darkness. . . . For God did not appoint us to suffer wrath but to receive salvation through our Lord Jesus Christ. (1 Thess. 5:2–5, 9)

In the midst of darkness, the Son of God shall gather all of God's earthly possessions, rescuing them from the coming wrath (which shall be delivered with the following seal).

In this apocalyptic time of complete darkness—under a blood-red moon—Earth will witness divine intervention like it hasn't seen since the first century A.D. Heaven's communication to Earth will be unmistakable: "[T]hat day will close . . . unexpectedly like a trap. For it will come upon all those who live on the face of the whole earth" (Luke 21:34, 35).

At that time [of the sixth seal] the kingdom of heaven will be like ten virgins who took their lamps and went out to meet the bridegroom. Five of them were foolish and five were wise. The foolish ones took their lamps but did not take any oil with them. The wise, however, took oil in jars along with their lamps. The bridegroom was a long time in coming, and they all became drowsy and fell asleep. At midnight the cry rang out: "Here's the bridegroom! Come out to meet him!" Then all the virgins woke up and trimmed their lamps. The foolish ones said to the wise, "Give us some of your oil; our lamps are going out." "No," they replied, "there may not be enough for both us and you. Instead, go to those who sell oil and buy some for yourselves." But while they were on their way to buy the oil, the bridegroom arrived. The virgins who were ready went in with him to the wedding banquet. And the door was shut. Later the others also came. "Sir! Sir!" they said. "Open the door for us!" But he replied, "I tell you the truth, I don't know you." Therefore keep watch, because you do not know the day or the hour. (Matt. 25:1–13)

In this parable, Jesus taught the following: to neglect the source of heavenly light is to forfeit what could have been. As the souls of the foolish were not illuminated when their Lord returned, they could not enter the banquet (in Heaven [Rev. 19:1–9]) and had to wait outside (on Earth). At the second coming of Christ, the opposing fates shall be delivered concurrently.

When the sixth seal does open, the course of history will be altered. Whereas the sixth seal announces the coming wrath, the seventh seal initiates its actual execution.

> When he opened the seventh seal, there was silence in heaven for about half an hour. And I saw the seven angels who

> stand before God, and to them were given seven trumpets. Another angel, who had a golden censer, came and stood at the altar. He was given much incense to offer, with the prayers of all the saints, on the golden altar before the throne. The smoke of the incense, together with the prayers of the saints, went up before God from the angel's hand. Then the angel took the censer, filled it with fire from the altar, and hurled it on the earth; and there came peals of thunder, rumblings, flashes of lightning and an earthquake. (Rev. 8:1–5)

The seventh seal sends a sweeping silence throughout the heavenly realm, for like a spiritual curtain, judgment shall now descend on planet Earth. An earthquake will literally shake the remaining population as a firestorm of thunder and lightning rages overhead. With these signs, the seven angels shall sound their trumpets, and one plague after another shall befall the world.

Events of the End: The Seven Seals of Christ's Prophecy

The first angel sounded his trumpet, and there came hail and fire mixed with blood, and it was hurled down upon the earth. A third of the earth was burned up, a third of the trees were burned up, and all the green grass was burned up. The second angel sounded his trumpet, and something like a huge mountain, all ablaze, was thrown into the sea. A third of the sea turned into blood, a third of the living creatures in the sea died, and a third of the ships were destroyed. The third angel sounded his trumpet, and a great star, blazing like a torch, fell from the sky on a third of the rivers and on the springs of water—the name of the star is Wormwood. A third of the waters turned bitter, and many people died from the waters that had become bitter. The fourth angel sounded his trumpet, and a third of the sun was struck, a third of the moon, and a third of the stars, so that a third of them turned dark. A third of the day was without light, and also a third of the night. As I watched, I heard an eagle that was flying in midair call

> out in a loud voice: "Woe! Woe! Woe to the inhabitants of the earth, because of the trumpet blasts about to be sounded by the other three angels!" (Rev. 8:7–13)

The plagued Earth shall resemble the days when Moses confronted Pharaoh in Egypt and "blood was everywhere" (Exod. 7:21). As wrath poured down upon Egypt, so it will upon the world when the trumpets sound.

With the fourth angel, time is marked by an eerie darkness that fills the planet; it is the omen that wrath shall grievously intensify. When the fifth, sixth, and seventh angels release their "woes," the global effects will be unprecedented.

> The fifth angel sounded his trumpet, and I saw a star [angel] that had fallen from the sky to the earth. The star was given the key to the shaft of the Abyss. When he opened the Abyss, smoke rose from it like the smoke from a gigantic furnace. The sun and sky were darkened by the smoke from the Abyss. And out of the smoke locusts came down

upon the earth and were given power like that of scorpions of the earth. They were told not to harm the grass of the earth or any plant or tree, but only those people who did not have the seal of God on their foreheads. They were not given power to kill them, but only to torture them for five months. And the agony they suffered was like that of the sting of a scorpion when it strikes a man. During those days men will seek death, but will not find it; they will long to die, but death will elude them. The locusts looked like horses prepared for battle. On their heads they wore something like crowns of gold, and their faces resembled human faces. Their hair was like women's hair, and their teeth were like lions' teeth. They had breastplates like breastplates of iron, and the sound of their wings was like the thundering of many horses and chariots rushing into battle. They had tails and stings like scorpions, and in their tails they had power to torment people for five months. They had as king over them the angel of the

> Abyss, whose name in Hebrew is Abaddon, and in Greek, Apollyon. The first woe is past; two other woes are yet to come. (Rev. 9:1–12)

From out of the bottomless pit, a demonic horde of vicious creatures shall assault the population (sparing only those "sealed" by God). Abaddon, who is the "destroyer" angel, shall rise to lead the attack.

Yet, just as the Israelites were spared in Egypt during the time of Pharaoh, so shall they be when Abaddon appears on the Earth's surface. He will not touch 144,000 of the twelve tribes, for after the sixth seal opens, they will be sealed by the angels: "I [John] heard the number of those who were sealed: 144,000 from all the tribes of Israel" (Rev. 7:4). (At a later point in time, they shall ascend to Heaven to be with Christ: "Then I [John] looked, and there before me was the Lamb, standing on Mount Zion, and with him 144,000 who had his name and his Father's name written on their foreheads [Rev. 14:1].)

The rest of the population shall endure their worst nightmare. Five months of anguish shall foment unstable emotions throughout the world, plunging the population into a desperate, chaotic state. It is then that Satan's angels will be unleashed.

> The sixth angel sounded his trumpet, and I heard a voice coming from the horns of the golden altar that is before God. It said to the sixth angel who had the trumpet, "Release the four angels who are bound at the great river Euphrates." And the four angels who had been kept ready for this very hour and day and month and year were released to kill a third of mankind. The number of the mounted troops was two hundred million. I heard their number. The horses and riders I saw in my vision looked like this: Their breastplates were fiery red, dark blue, and yellow as sulfur. The heads of the horses resembled the heads of lions, and out of their mouths came fire, smoke and sulfur. A third of mankind was killed by

> the three plagues of fire, smoke and sulfur that came out of their mouths. The power of the horses was in their mouths and in their tails; for their tails were like snakes, having heads with which they inflict injury. The rest of mankind that were not killed by these plagues still did not repent of the work of their hands; they did not stop worshiping demons, and idols of gold, silver, bronze, stone and wood—idols that cannot see or hear or walk. Nor did they repent of their murders, their magic arts, their sexual immorality or their thefts. (Rev. 9:13–21)

Four evil angels will channel the power of darkness, driving a ruthless army of two hundred million "mounted troops" to deliver death. Those left in the world will face three and a half years of unrelenting plagues, for two prophets of God—who shall testify to Heaven's power—shall rise to execute judgment.

"And I will give power to my two witnesses, and they will prophesy for 1,260 days, clothed in sackcloth." These are the two olive trees and the two lampstands that stand before the Lord of the earth. If anyone tries to harm them, fire comes from their mouths and devours their enemies. This is how anyone who wants to harm them must die. These men have power to shut up the sky so that it will not rain during the time they are prophesying; and they have power to turn the waters into blood and to strike the earth with every kind of plague as often as they want. Now when they have finished their testimony, the beast [the Antichrist] that comes up from the Abyss will attack them, and overpower and kill them. Their bodies will lie in the street of the great city, which is figuratively called Sodom and Egypt, where also their Lord was crucified. For three and a half days men from every people, tribe, language and nation will gaze on their bodies and refuse them burial. The inhabitants of the earth will gloat over them and will celebrate by sending each other gifts, because these two prophets had tormented those who live on the earth. But after the three and a half days a breath of life from God entered them, and they stood on their feet, and terror struck those who saw them. Then they heard a loud voice from heaven saying to them, "Come up here." And they went up to heaven in a cloud, while their enemies looked on. At that very hour there was a severe earthquake and a tenth of the city collapsed. Seven thousand people were killed in the earthquake, and the survivors were terrified and gave glory to the God of heaven. The second woe has passed; the third woe is coming soon. (Rev. 11:3–14)

These prophets shall strike the unrepentant population with plagues as often as they command. Yet, like Christ, they shall be killed. The Antichrist shall end their lives and their plagues. He will parade their dead bodies through the streets of the "dark" city (now called "Sodom and Egypt"), and the evil inhabitants will find their "salvation" in the false savior.

With the death and ascension of the prophets, the globe is now on the cusp of a new order—world domination by the Antichrist. However, before the apostle John witnesses the vision of this final woe, he sees the Ark of the Covenant in the temple of God.

> Then God's temple in heaven was opened, and within his temple was seen the ark of his covenant. And there came flashes of lightning, rumblings, peals of thunder, an earthquake and a great hailstorm. (Rev. 11:19)

Upon seeing the source of all righteousness, John then witnessed the signs that mark complete unrighteousness—the third woe, the rise of the beast.

> And I saw a beast [the Antichrist] coming out of the sea. He had ten horns and seven heads, with ten crowns on his

horns, and on each head a blasphemous name. The beast I saw resembled a leopard, but had feet like those of a bear and a mouth like that of a lion. The dragon [Satan] gave the beast his power and his throne and great authority. One of the heads of the beast seemed to have had a fatal wound, but the fatal wound had been healed. The whole world was astonished and followed the beast. Men worshiped the dragon because he had given authority to the beast, and they also worshiped the beast and asked, "Who is like the beast? Who can make war against him?" The beast was given a mouth to utter proud words and blasphemies and to exercise his authority for forty-two months. He opened his mouth to blaspheme God, and to slander his name and his dwelling place and those who live in heaven. He was given power to make war against the saints [the twelve tribes] and to conquer them. And he was given authority over every tribe, people, language and nation. All inhabitants of the earth will worship the

> beast—all whose names have not been written in the book of life belonging to the Lamb that was slain from the creation of the world. (Rev. 13:1–8)

Through deceit and spiritual power, the false savior shall bring order to the spiritually dark planet. This counterfeit Christ shall unite the deceived population, consolidating all secular and religious power under his hand. The darkest impulses of demonic passion shall be demonstrated—without limits—by a soul lost to Satan. Infused with spiritual energy, the beast shall recover from a mortal wound and deify himself.

As supreme dictator, the Antichrist will rule from his temple, ushering in the new dark age of man. All religions will cease as the false savior proclaims himself to be *the* one true God:

> He [the Antichrist] will oppose and will exalt himself over everything that is called God or is worshiped, so that he

> sets himself up in God's temple, proclaiming himself to be God.... The coming of the lawless one [the Antichrist] will be in accordance with the work of Satan displayed in all kinds of counterfeit miracles, signs and wonders, and in every sort of evil that deceives those who are perishing. They perish because they refused to love the truth and so be saved. (2 Thess. 2:4, 9, 10)

Where once prophets of God spoke words of light, the Antichrist shall spew forth vile propaganda and glorify himself. Through the use of "counterfeit miracles," the "lawless one" will successfully deceive the population because they "refused to love the truth." The ungodly inhabitants had "no reverence for sacred things" and not only were "irreligious" but also practiced the "opposite" of righteousness.[3] They rejected God's "royal invitation" to enter his kingdom and did not know God because they refused to "recognize him."[4]

As disciples of the Antichrist, the subservient population shall also be in subjec-

Events of the End:
The Seven Seals of Christ's Prophecy

tion to the second beast. Known as the false prophet, this mouthpiece for Satan shall establish and enforce the one-world religion.

> Then I [John] saw another beast, coming out of the earth. He had two horns like a lamb, but he spoke like a dragon. He exercised all the authority of the first beast on his behalf, and made the earth and its inhabitants worship the first beast, whose fatal wound had been healed. And he performed great and miraculous signs, even causing fire to come down from heaven to earth in full view of men. Because of the signs he was given power to do on behalf of the first beast, he deceived the inhabitants of the earth. He ordered them to set up an image in honor of the beast who was wounded by the sword and yet lived. He was given power to give breath to the image of the first beast, so that it could speak and cause all who refused to worship the image to be killed. He also forced everyone, small and great, rich and poor, free and slave, to receive a mark on his right

> hand or on his forehead, so that no one could buy or sell unless he had the mark, which is the name of the beast or the number of his name. This calls for wisdom. If anyone has insight, let him calculate the number of the beast, for it is man's number. His number is 666. (Rev. 13:11–18)

When the population bends its knee to a talking idol and worships the Antichrist as God, the angel of darkness will revel in the power of deception. With the world enslaved to his will, Satan will now oppose Heaven without restraint.

Allured by illusion, souls on Earth will relinquish their hearts to darkness and their minds to the religious order. As cogs in a wheel of slavery and death, their lives will be consumed with fear and evil; the worldwide inquisition shall produce martyrs or abject servitude. Those who choose to make a covenant with Satan shall be sealed with a permanent seal—branded with the number of the beast's name: "666." Thereby, their fate cannot be altered.

> If anyone worships the beast and his image and receives his mark on the forehead or on the hand, he, too, will drink of the wine of God's fury, which has been poured full strength into the cup of his wrath. He will be tormented with burning sulfur in the presence of the holy angels and of the Lamb. And the smoke of their torment rises for ever and ever. There is no rest day or night for those who worship the beast and his image, or for anyone who receives the mark of his name. (Rev. 14:9–11)

This prophecy of judgment will come to pass when the seven angels unleash the final plagues.

> I [John] saw in heaven another great and marvelous sign: seven angels with the seven last plagues—last, because with them God's wrath is completed. . . . Then I heard a loud voice from the temple saying to the seven angels, "Go, pour out the seven bowls of God's wrath on the earth."

The first angel went and poured out his bowl on the land, and ugly and painful sores broke out on the people who had the mark of the beast and worshiped his image.

The second angel poured out his bowl on the sea, and it turned into blood like that of a dead man, and every living thing in the sea died.

The third angel poured out his bowl on the rivers and springs of water, and they became blood. Then I heard the angel in charge of the waters say: "You are just in these judgments, you who are and who were, the Holy One, because you have so judged; for they have shed the blood of your saints and prophets, and you have given them blood to drink as they deserve."

The fourth angel poured out his bowl on the sun, and the sun was given power to scorch people with fire. They were seared by the intense heat and they cursed the name of God, who had control over these plagues, but they refused to repent and glorify him.

> The fifth angel poured out his bowl on the throne of the beast, and his kingdom was plunged into darkness. Men gnawed their tongues in agony and cursed the God of heaven because of their pains and their sores, but they refused to repent of what they had done.
>
> The sixth angel poured out his bowl on the great river Euphrates, and its water was dried up to prepare the way for the kings from the East. Then I saw three evil spirits that looked like frogs; they came out of the mouth of the dragon, out of the mouth of the beast and out of the mouth of the false prophet. They are spirits of demons performing miraculous signs, and they go out to the kings of the whole world, to gather them for the battle on the great day of God Almighty. . . . Then they gathered the kings together to the place that in Hebrew is called Armageddon. (Rev. 15:1; 16:1–6, 8–14, 16)

With the evaporation of the Euphrates River, the kings of the East will sweep into the

Middle East to Armageddon. ("Armageddon is a compound word that means 'mountain of Megiddo.' . . . All major traffic through northern Palestine traveled past Megiddo, making it a strategic military stronghold."⁵)

However, like every evil army that has cursed the globe, these warriors are nothing more than pawns on the chessboard, wasted souls without hope. Divine prophecy is against them.

> They [the ten kings] will make war against the Lamb, but the Lamb will overcome them because he is Lord of lords and King of kings—and with him will be his called, chosen and faithful followers [the kingdom of Christ]. (Rev. 17:14)

The King of kings shall obliterate ten of Satan's kings. No armament made in this world will be able to withstand the power that Christ shall bring from Heaven. At the battle of Armageddon, the true Christ shall annihilate the children of darkness, forever separating them from the glory and strength of the Most High.

> [T]he Lord Jesus shall be revealed from heaven with his mighty angels, In flaming fire taking vengeance on them that know not God, and that obey not the gospel of our Lord Jesus Christ: Who shall be punished with everlasting destruction from the presence of the Lord, and from the glory of his power. (2 Thess. 1:7–9 KJV)

The Son of God prophesied of this apocalyptic time, comparing it to the horrific destruction that fell upon Sodom and Gomorrah.

> It was the same in the days of Lot. People were eating and drinking, buying and selling, planting and building. But the day Lot left Sodom, fire and sulfur rained down from heaven and destroyed them all. It will be just like this on the day the Son of Man is revealed. (Luke 17:28–30)

After two angels rescued a righteous man named Lot from Sodom, flaming sulfur poured down upon the cities, burying everything in its fiery wake.

(Just as renowned as the story itself has been the archaeological quest to determine whether these fabled cities truly ever existed. Throughout the twentieth century, archaeologists dug in the sands along the shore of the Dead Sea and uncovered a wealth of knowledge—buried for over 4,000 years. What they discovered were the ruins of two ancient neighbors: Bab edh Dhra and Numeira. Carbon 14 dating revealed that these sister cities were destroyed at the same point in history, succumbing to a violent, fiery end. Bones found under collapsed walls indicate that the inhabitants were caught in the middle of a traumatic finish. Because there are no volcanoes in the area, scientists have ruled out a volcanic eruption as the cause of the destruction.

Pottery found among the ruins dates the cities to the early Bronze Age: 3300 to 2050 B.C. Scholars agree that if Sodom and

Gomorrah existed, it would have been during this time frame. Hence, archaeologists found two sister cities identified to be in the correct biblical location at the right place in time. The overwhelming amount of evidence compelled archaeologists to set forth the following theory: Bab edh Dhra is Sodom and Numeira is Gomorrah.)

Just as the unsuspecting inhabitants of the morally bankrupt cities reaped the consequences of their actions, so shall those in the Antichrist's kingdom when Christ is "revealed" (*Apokalupsis* in the Greek language). This prophecy shall be fulfilled after the seventh angel smites the planet with the final plague.

> The seventh angel poured out his bowl into the air, and out of the temple came a loud voice from the throne, saying, "It is done!" Then there came flashes of lightning, rumblings, peals of thunder and a severe earthquake. No earthquake like it has ever occurred since man has been on earth, so tremendous was

> the quake. The great city split into three parts, and the cities of the nations collapsed. God remembered Babylon the Great and gave her the cup filled with the wine of the fury of his wrath. Every island fled away and the mountains could not be found. From the sky huge hailstones of about a hundred pounds each fell upon men. And they cursed God on account of the plague of hail, because the plague was so terrible. (Rev. 16:17–21)

With thunder and lightning saturating the sky, a catastrophic earthquake will send fissures rippling throughout the planet. Every island shall slide into the sea, and mountain ranges shall collapse. With his empire literally crumbling, the Antichrist will witness his capital split in three directions. Earth itself shall tear at the very foundation of his throne.

The inhabitants marked by the beast are trapped in the world they conquered. While they are being bombarded with hail stones, the pitiful survivors will shake their fists at God, blaming him instead of placing blame where it belongs—on themselves and their wickedness.

This cataclysmic event marks time. The Apocalypse is at the door. Christ will descend out of Heaven and shall be victorious—when the armies of Heaven fight against the armies of Earth.

> I [John] saw heaven standing open and there before me was a white horse, whose rider is called Faithful and True. With justice he judges and makes war. His eyes are like blazing fire, and on his head are many crowns. He has a name written on him that no one knows but he himself. He is dressed in a robe dipped in blood, and his name is the Word of God. The armies of heaven were following him, riding on white horses and dressed in fine linen, white and clean. Out of his mouth comes a sharp sword with which to strike down the nations. "He will rule them with an iron scepter." He treads the winepress of the fury of the wrath of God Al-

mighty. On his robe and on his thigh he has this name written:

KING OF KINGS AND LORD OF LORDS.

And I saw an angel standing in the sun, who cried in a loud voice to all the birds flying in midair, "Come, gather together for the great supper of God, so that you may eat the flesh of kings, generals, and mighty men, of horses and their riders, and the flesh of all people, free and slave, small and great." Then I saw the beast and the kings of the earth and their armies gathered together to make war against the rider on the horse and his army. But the beast was captured, and with him the false prophet who had performed the miraculous signs on his behalf. With these signs he had deluded those who had received the mark of the beast and worshiped his image. The two of them were thrown alive into the fiery lake of burning sulfur. The rest of them were killed with the sword that came out of the mouth of the rider on the horse, and all the birds gorged themselves on their flesh. (Rev. 19:11–21)

God's King will overtake Satan's king. With the Apocalypse, the beast and false prophet will be forever enslaved by liquefied sulfur, their army will become a feast for the birds, and Satan will be imprisoned in the bottomless pit.

> And I saw an angel coming down out of heaven, having the key to the Abyss and holding in his hand a great chain. He seized the dragon, that ancient serpent, who is the devil, or Satan, and bound him for a thousand years. He threw him into the Abyss, and locked and sealed it over him, to keep him from deceiving the nations anymore until the thousand years were ended. After that, he must be set free for a short time. (Rev. 20:1–3)

With the dark angel imprisoned in the Abyss, a resurrection of the dead will follow; all souls martyred during the beast's reign shall rise from the grave.

> I saw the souls of those who had been beheaded because of their testimony for Jesus and because of the word of God. They had not worshiped the beast or his image and had not received his mark on their foreheads or their hands. They came to life and reigned with Christ a thousand years. (The rest of the dead did not come to life until the thousand years were ended.) This is the first resurrection. Blessed and holy are those who have part in the first resurrection. The second death has no power over them, but they will be priests of God and of Christ and will reign with him for a thousand years. (Rev. 20:4–6)

From the ashes of Armageddon, a new thousand-year kingdom shall rise upon the Earth, and the resurrected martyrs will reign with Christ. At that time, the Creator will "restore the fortunes of Judah and Jerusalem" (Joel 3:1).

As Moses delivered the Israelites from the hand of Pharaoh, so will the Messiah deliver remnants of the twelve tribes from the grip of the Antichrist. ("If those days [of the beast] had not been cut short, no one would survive, but for the sake of the elect [the twelve tribes] those days will be shortened [by the Apocalypse]" Matt. 24:22.)

The deliverer of the twelve tribes shall preside over the new kingdom in Jerusalem during a time of unprecedented peace. "Freedom from satanic interference and immediate divine rule will make it the most ideal period of world history since the fall of man."[6]

While the resurrected martyrs reign with Christ in his millennial kingdom, the imprisoned dragon will remain chained in the Abyss. However, this separation between righteousness and unrighteousness is only temporary, for Satan will be released from his shackles and will pursue one last attempt to destroy God's people. His final move against Heaven, however, brings checkmate.

> When the thousand years are over, Satan will be released from his prison and will go out to deceive the nations in

> the four corners of the earth—Gog and Magog—to gather them for battle. In number they are like the sand on the seashore. They marched across the breadth of the earth and surrounded the camp of God's people [the twelve tribes], the city he loves [Jerusalem]. But fire came down from heaven and devoured them. And the devil, who deceived them, was thrown into the lake of burning sulfur, where the beast and the false prophet had been thrown. They will be tormented day and night for ever and ever. (Rev. 20:7–10)

In the lake of fire, Satan shall remember the justice of Heaven forever. The calamity he brought upon creation shall be upon him without end.

His army shall know immediate death. Called "Gog and Magog" because it is the embodiment of ancient evil, the army shall fall to the will of Heaven, the evil it brought shall be forever expunged, and divine prophecy will be fulfilled (Ezek. 38). Never again shall Satan's darkness arise to afflict the righteous.

Following this threshold in time, the second resurrection of the seventh seal will come to pass. All souls not raised during the previous resurrections—righteous and unrighteous—shall hear the voice of Christ: "[A] time is coming when all who are in their graves will hear his voice and come out—those who have done good will rise to live, and those who have done evil will rise to be condemned" (John 5:28, 29). Christ expounded upon this prophecy by way of the vision he gave to John.

> Then I saw a great white throne and him who was seated on it. Earth and sky fled from his presence, and there was no place for them. And I saw the dead, great and small, standing before the throne, and books were opened. Another book was opened, which is the book of life. The dead were judged according to what they had done as recorded in the books. The sea gave up the dead that were in it,

> and death and Hades gave up the dead that were in them, and each person was judged according to what he had done. Then death and Hades were thrown into the lake of fire. The lake of fire is the second death. If anyone's name was not found written in the book of life, he was thrown into the lake of fire. (Rev. 20:11–15)

From the center of the great white throne, Christ shall judge. Those souls who are "blotted out of the book of life and not . . . listed with the righteous" (Ps. 69:28), will die a second death. Never shall their souls live again. In contrast, any soul found in the book of life shall live to see paradise. Those souls resurrected unto eternal life will join the martyred souls (raised after the fifth and seventh seals), the kingdom of Christ (raised after the sixth), and the "144,000."

This is the prophecy of Judgment Day.

> When the Son of Man comes in his glory, and all the angels with him, he will

sit on his throne in heavenly glory. All the nations will be gathered before him, and he will separate the people one from another as a shepherd separates the sheep from the goats. He will put the sheep on his right and the goats on his left. Then the King will say to those on his right, "Come, you who are blessed by my Father; take your inheritance, the kingdom prepared for you since the creation of the world." . . . Then he will say to those on his left, "Depart from me, you who are cursed, into the eternal fire prepared for the devil and his angels." . . . Then they will go away to eternal punishment, but the righteous to eternal life. (Matt. 25:31–34, 41, 46)

This is the end: the permanent separation of light from darkness. Desperation awaits those who are sentenced to the "second death," whereas unlimited love and freedom await the righteous. This prophecy of judgment marks not only the permanent divide between Heaven and "hell," but also the transition between this world and the next.

> Lift up your eyes to the heavens, look at the earth beneath; the heavens will vanish like smoke, the earth will wear out like a garment. (Isa. 51:6)

> [T]he heavens shall pass away with a great noise, and the elements shall melt with fervent heat, the earth also and the works that are therein shall be burned up.... [And] we, according to his promise, look for new heavens and a new earth, wherein dwelleth righteousness. (2 Peter 3:10, 13 KJV)

> The former things will not be remembered, nor will they come to mind. (Isa. 65:17)

When the molecular bonds in the atmospheric heavens melt in a ferocious inferno, this creation shall roar out of existence, ushering in the new age where evil will not exist nor be remembered.

Events of the End: The Seven Seals of Christ's Prophecy

Visions of this new creation—the most intriguing scenes ever revealed—were given to the apostle John.

> Then I saw a new heaven and a new earth, for the first heaven and the first earth had passed away, and there was no longer any sea. I saw the Holy City, the new Jerusalem, coming down out of heaven from God, prepared as a bride beautifully dressed for her husband. And I heard a loud voice from the throne saying, "Now the dwelling of God is with men, and he will live with them. They will be his people, and God himself will be with them and be their God. He will wipe every tear from their eyes. There will be no more death or mourning or crying or pain, for the old order of things has passed away."
>
> He who was seated on the throne said, "I am making everything new!" Then he said,
>
> "Write this down, for these words are trustworthy and true." . . . "He who overcomes will inherit all this, and I will

be his God and he will be my son." . . . And he [the angel] carried me away in the Spirit to a mountain great and high, and showed me the Holy City, Jerusalem, coming down out of heaven from God. It shone with the glory of God, and its brilliance was like that of a very precious jewel, like a jasper, clear as crystal. It had a great, high wall with twelve gates, and with twelve angels at the gates. . . . The twelve gates were twelve pearls, each gate made of a single pearl. The great street of the city was of pure gold, like transparent glass. I did not see a temple in the city, because the Lord God Almighty and the Lamb are its temple. The city does not need the sun or the moon to shine on it, for the glory of God gives it light, and the Lamb is its lamp. The nations will walk by its light, and the kings of the earth will bring their splendor into it. On no day will its gates ever be shut, for there will be no night there. The glory and honor of the nations will be brought into it. (Rev. 21:1–5, 7, 10–12, 21–26)

Events of the End:
The Seven Seals of Christ's Prophecy

> Then the angel showed me the river of the water of life, as clear as crystal, flowing from the throne of God and of the Lamb down the middle of the great street of the city. On each side of the river stood the tree of life, bearing twelve crops of fruit, yielding its fruit every month. And the leaves of the tree are for the healing of the nations. No longer will there be any curse. The throne of God and of the Lamb will be in the city, and his servants will serve him. They will see his face, and his name will be on their foreheads. There will be no more night. They will not need the light of a lamp or the light of the sun, for the Lord God will give them light. And they will reign for ever and ever. (Rev. 22:1–5)

In the new world, space and time will be redefined. Time's marking will expand beyond human comprehension. "With the Lord a day is like a thousand years, and a thousand years are like a day" (2 Peter 3:8). No longer will time reflect the placement of sun, moon, and stars because no sun will exist to light the new Earth; Heaven's glorious majesty shall illuminate it. Eternal souls will continue forward in an elevated state of awareness, in a permanent state of peace. Utopia—a system of perfect social interaction—waits on the other side.

The Son of God described life in the new age by contrasting it with life in this world:

> The people of this age marry and are given in marriage. But those who are considered worthy of taking part in that age and in the resurrection from the dead will neither marry nor be given in marriage, and they can no longer die; for they are like the angels. They are God's children, since they are children of the resurrection. (Luke 20:34–36)

"In the new age there will be no marriage, no procreation and no death."[7] The "children of the resurrection" shall dwell in a world that transcends the boundaries of human imagination. In the new age, the spirits of righteous men shall be as angels in the city of the living God, Zion, the holy city that shall descend from above, crowning the new home of mankind.

The prophecy states that when finite time stops, eternity unfolds.

> [Y]ou have come to Mount Zion, to the heavenly Jerusalem, the city of the living God. You have come to thousands upon thousands of angels in joyful assembly, to the church of the firstborn, whose names are written in heaven. You have come to God, the judge of all men, to the spirits of righteous men made perfect. (Heb. 12:22, 23)

3

THE SEVENTIETH "SEVEN"

> Then the sovereignty, power and greatness of the kingdoms under the whole heaven will be handed over to the saints, the people of the Most High.
>
> —The Prophet Daniel (Dan. 7:27)

Centuries before Christ, the angel Gabriel gave revelation to the prophet Daniel regarding the future of Israel's twelve tribes. Gabriel spoke of three significant events: the restoration of Jerusalem, the crucifixion of the Messiah, and the future covenant with Daniel's people.

The angel pinned the first two events along a time line. In his prophecy, Gabriel did not specify years on the calendar, but he marked time by seven-year increments, referring to them as "sevens." Seven "sevens" would mark the first phase of the prophecy (Jerusalem's restoration would take forty-nine years to complete), and sixty-two "sevens" would mark the second phase (Jesus' Crucifixion would occur 434 years later).

With the first two events of Gabriel's prophecy already complete, only the final "seven" remains. When the seventieth "seven" is fulfilled, then the new kingdom for the twelve tribes shall become reality. The fulfillment of the seventieth "seven" though will not occur until after the second coming of Christ to gather his kingdom.

Until the Lord's return, Earth remains in the block of time between the sixty-ninth "seven" (which was fulfilled in first century), and seventieth "seven" (which has yet to commence). Jesus Christ himself identified this time span, referring to it as the "times of the Gentiles" (Luke 21:24). It represents a piece of man's history that is unprecedented: all bloodlines can receive eternal life through the Messiah.

The Son of God marked this gap in time—at the synagogue in Nazareth—when he referenced the following prophecy given by the prophet Isaiah:

> The Spirit of the Sovereign Lord is on me, because the Lord has anointed me to preach good news to the poor. He has sent me to bind up the brokenhearted, to proclaim freedom for the captives and release from darkness for the prisoners, to proclaim the year of the Lord's favor [fulfilled in the first century] and the day of vengeance of our God [to be fulfilled via the Apocalypse].(Isa. 61:1, 2)

When the Son of God read this from the scroll of Isaiah, he closed the scroll after he read "to proclaim the year of the Lord's favor." He never read "and the day of vengeance of our God," for that time would come at a *future* point in time—fulfilled during the seventieth "seven." He stopped after reading "the year of the Lord's favor" because it applied *his* day and time: the sixty-ninth "seven." Herein, Christ marked the gap in time when he read from this scroll(Luke 4:18, 19). His first coming to Earth would fulfill the first part of Isaiah's prophecy ("the Lord's favor"), and his Apocalypse would fulfill the second part ("vengeance"). Between the two parts—between the "sevens"—is the block of time that we are currently in: the "times of the Gentiles."

Like Jesus, the prophet Joel identified this unique time in history. He spoke of the signs that would mark its commencement and the signs that would mark the return of Christ to gather his kingdom.

> I will pour out my Spirit on all people. Your sons and daughters will prophesy, your old men will dream dreams, your young men will see visions.

> Even on my servants, both men and women, I will pour out my Spirit in those days. I will show wonders in the heavens and on the earth, blood and fire and billows of smoke. The sun will be turned to darkness and the moon to blood before the coming of the great and dreadful day of the Lord. And everyone who calls on the name of the Lord will be saved. (Joel 2:28–32)

Anyone who calls on the name of the Lord during the times of the Gentiles will awaken to immortality at the second coming of Christ. Once the kingdom of Christ is gathered from this world, then Gabriel's prophecy of the seventieth "seven" will (soon) follow.

Whereas Gabriel outlined the final "seven," Christ elucidated the nature of it: the seventieth "seven" is the seven-year countdown to Armageddon.

Seven years before the Apocalypse, the sixth trumpet shall sound, and the prophets of God shall smite the planet for three and a half years. With the seventh trumpet, Satan's beast shall smite the population for the next three and a half years. Hence, together, the prophets of Heaven and "hell" make up the final prophecy given by Gabriel. In essence, the seventieth "seven" is a prelude to war. With the Apocalypse and Armageddon, Gabriel's trilogy will be fulfilled.

This epic prophecy, given by Gabriel and recorded by Daniel, is disclosed here.

> While I [Daniel] was speaking and praying, confessing my sin and the sin of my people Israel and making my request to the Lord my God for his holy hill—while I was still in prayer, Gabriel, the man I had seen in the earlier vision, came to me in swift flight about the time of the evening sacrifice. He instructed me and said to me, "Daniel, I have now come to give you insight and understanding. As soon as you began to pray, an answer was given, which I have come to tell you, for you are highly esteemed. Therefore, consider the message and understand the vision:

The Seventieth "Seven"

"Seventy 'sevens' are decreed for your people[1] and your holy city to finish transgression, to put an end to sin, to atone for wickedness, to bring in everlasting righteousness, to seal up vision and prophecy and to anoint the most holy.

"Know and understand this: From the issuing of the decree to restore and rebuild Jerusalem until the Anointed One, the ruler, comes, there will be seven 'sevens,' and sixty-two 'sevens.' It [Jerusalem] will be rebuilt with streets and a trench, but in times of trouble. After the sixty-two 'sevens,' the Anointed One will be cut off [Christ will be crucified] and will have nothing. The people of the ruler who will come will destroy the city [Jerusalem] and the sanctuary. The end will come like a flood: War will continue until the end, and desolations have been decreed. He will confirm a covenant with many [Israelites] for one 'seven' [the seventieth]. In the middle of the 'seven' [after three and a half years] he will put an end to sacrifice and offering [at this time, the two prophets of God will be killed].

> And on a wing of the temple [in Jerusalem] he will set up an abomination that causes desolation [the Antichrist], until the end that is decreed is poured out on him [at the Apocalypse]." (Dan. 9:20–27)

> Then the sovereignty, power and greatness of the kingdoms under the whole heaven will be handed over to the saints, the people of the Most High. (Dan. 7:27)

The seventieth "seven" will be fulfilled when the Son of God returns like "lightning" out of Heaven (Luke 17:24). Then the millennial kingdom of Christ will commence, which the Lord God himself spoke of long before the first century dawned:

> I [God] will create Jerusalem to be a delight and its people a joy. I will rejoice over Jerusalem and take delight in my people; the sound of weeping and of crying will be heard in it no more. Never again will there be in it an infant who lives but a few days, or an old man who does

not live out his years; he who dies at a hundred will be thought a mere youth; he who fails to reach a hundred will be considered accursed. They will build houses and dwell in them; they will plant vineyards and eat their fruit. No longer will they build houses and others live in them, or plant and others eat. For as the days of a tree, so will be the days of my people; my chosen ones will long enjoy the works of their hands. They will not toil in vain or bear children doomed to misfortune; for they will be a people blessed by the Lord, they and their descendants with them. Before they call I will answer; while they are still speaking I will hear. (Isa. 65:18–24)

This is the time prophesied by the angel Gabriel. His prophecy had not only marked the start of the New Covenant (fulfilled with the sixty-ninth "seven"), but it also had marked the start of Christ's millennial kingdom (fulfilled with the seventieth "seven").

However, Christ's millennial kingdom will not arise, the Apocalypse will not happen, and the Antichrist will not rule until all the souls who call upon the name of the Lord first ascend off this planet. Satan's kingdom of consummate darkness (which precedes God's kingdom of absolute light), cannot subjugate the world until the Spirit of Christ exits the Earth.

While the Spirit of Christ continues to be present, the spirit of Antichrist cannot rise in the beast. This is why the counterfeit Christ has yet to assume power—he will be revealed in his time. Therein, modern prophecies that speculate on the Antichrist's identity are without scriptural justification. The beast will not be revealed until after the sixth seal opens, when the Spirit of Christ is "taken out of the way."

> And now you know what is holding him [the Antichrist] back, so that he may be revealed at the proper time. For the secret power of lawlessness is already at work; but the one [God] who

The Seventieth "Seven"

> now holds it back will continue to do so till he [Christ] is taken out of the way [when he ascends with the spiritual harvest]. And then the lawlessness one [the Antichrist] will be revealed, whom the Lord Jesus will overthrow with the breath of his mouth and destroy by the splendor of his coming [via the Apocalypse]. (2 Thess. 2:6–8)

When the seventh trumpet sounds, then the "secret" power of Satan will finally manifest itself in the person of the Antichrist. Only through the ascension with Christ can a soul be separated from this fate.

At this current moment in time, the sands of time are draining on the invitation to enter Christ's kingdom. When time runs out, the sixth seal will open and the course of history will be forever altered. Like the flooding rains that fell to Earth during Noah's day, Christ's second coming will appear at an unknown moment in time. This is the prophecy given by the Son of God:

No one knows about that day or hour [of the sixth seal], not even the angels in heaven, nor the Son, but only the Father. As it was in the days of Noah, so it will be at the coming of the Son of Man. For in the days before the flood, people were eating and drinking, marrying and giving in marriage, up to the day Noah entered the ark; and they knew nothing about what would happen until the flood came and took them all away. That is how it will be at the coming of the Son of Man. Two men will be in the field; one will be taken [to be with Christ] and the other left [behind]. Two women will be grinding with a hand mill; one will be taken and the other left. Therefore keep watch, because you do not know on what day your Lord will come. (Matt. 24:36–42)

4

THE CODE OF PSALMS

O Lord my God, thou art very great; thou art clothed with honour and majesty. Who coverest *thyself* with light as *with* a garment: who stretchest out the heavens like a curtain: Who layeth the beams of his chambers in the waters: who maketh the clouds his chariot: who walketh upon the wings of the wind.

—King David (Ps. 104:1–3 KJV)

As the prophet Daniel marked the first coming of Christ, there is a prophet who marked the second coming of Christ; as the sixty-nine "sevens" were marked in time, so, too, is the seventieth "seven" marked in time, for there is a biblical code that reveals when these end-time events shall be fulfilled. By way of divine revelation supplied in this chapter, we will witness the following: The *history* of the *twentieth* century is prophecy fulfilled, and *prophecy* that pertains to the *twenty-first* century is history in the making.

We begin this study on the timing of prophetic statements by first looking to what Christ said regarding divine prophecy: "Everything must be fulfilled that is written about me in the Law of Moses, the Prophets and the Psalms" (Luke 24:44). Hence, we have divine revelation from the Messiah revealing that throughout the Old Testament, there are prophetic statements about him.

As we look at the three classifications cited by the Messiah, the one that stands unique is the Psalms; the Law of Moses consists of five separate books, the prophets are many in number, but the Psalms is one book (that is composed of five individual "books" totaling 150 Psalms). Christ himself marked the significance of the Psalms and their relation to end-time events when, in the Book of Revelation, he spoke of the "key of David" (Rev. 3:7). This "key of David" opens the door to the Davidic prophecy recorded in the Psalms, and "what he [Christ] opens [with that key] no one can shut" (Rev. 3:7).

To delve into the depth of what the Psalms communicate, the following must first be noted: "Moses gave to the Israelites the five books of the Law; and corresponding with these David gave them the five books of the Psalms."[1] In essence, the five books within the Psalms correlate with the five books of Moses. "They, in turn, present an outline of future events. A Genesis period (Psalms 1–41) was predicted for the land of Palestine to be prepared for the Chosen

People. An Exodus period (Psalms 42–72) was predicted when the Chosen People would return to their land. A Leviticus period (Psalms 73–89) was predicted for the restoration of Temple worship. A Numbers period (Psalms 90–106) was predicted for the world to suffer unparalleled tribulation. Finally, a Deuteronomy period (Psalms 106–150) was predicted for the Messiah to establish the kingdom."[2]

Clearly, the Psalms address the twelve tribes of Israel, are prophetic in nature, and correspond to a defined sequence in time. The question is: Where in time are these prophecies found?

We begin with the following fundamental picture: Old and New Testament prophecies foretold the return of the twelve tribes (the Jews) to the Holy Land; the formation of Israel in the twentieth century marked the fulfillment of those prophecies. With this understanding, we shall see the following: Psalms 1–150 correlate with the calendar years of the twentieth and twenty-first centuries. Herein, we shall find the history of the twelve tribes in the twentieth century, and prophecies of their future in the twenty-first—written in the Psalms.

We'll begin by examining four pivotal points in history for the twelve tribes: World War II (1939–1945), the Gulf War (1991), "Jerusalem 3000" (the 1996 celebration that marked the 3000th anniversary of King David bringing the Ark of the Covenant to Jerusalem), and finally, the establishment of Israel (1948). We'll step back in time and find the correlations in the corresponding Psalms, which reveal prophetic statements that are connected to our reality.

During World War II, the twelve tribes went into captivity under Nazi Germany; we'll focus on the last three years of the war by looking to Psalms 43–45: "Vindicate me, O God, and plead my cause against an ungodly nation [Germany]; rescue me from deceitful and wicked men [the Nazis]" (Ps. 43:1) "My disgrace is before me all day long [in the concentration camps], and my face is covered with shame at the taunts of those who reproach and revile me, because of the enemy, who is bent on revenge" (Ps. 44:15, 16). "They [the twelve tribes] are led in with joy and gladness [out of captivity]; they enter the palace of the king. Your sons will take the place of your fathers [to be gathered again in the Holy Land]; you will make them princes throughout the land. I [God] will perpetuate your memory through all generations; therefore the nations will praise you for ever and ever [a prophecy of freedom and hope, which includes looking to the millennial kingdom]" (Ps. 45:15–17). The dread of 1943 and 1944 turned into deliverance and hope in 1945.

Forty-six years after World War II ended, the Gulf War erupted. The poetic writings found in Psalm 91 mark a war where flesh and blood weaponry is unleashed alongside divine intervention.

> He who dwells in the shelter of the Most High will rest in the shadow of the Almighty. I will say of the Lord, "He is my refuge and my fortress, my God, in

whom I trust." Surely he will save you from the fowler's snare [Iraq] and from the deadly pestilence [chemical warfare]. He will cover you with his feathers, and under his wings [aircraft] you will find refuge; his faithfulness will be your shield and rampart [military defense]. You will not fear the terror of night, nor the arrow [SCUD missiles] that flies by day, nor the pestilence [unseen biological poison] that stalks in the darkness, nor the plague that destroys at midday. A thousand [enemy soldiers] may fall at your side, ten thousand at your right hand, but it will not come near you. You will only observe with your eyes [Israel would not engage in the conflict] and see the punishment of the wicked. If you make the Most High your dwelling—even the Lord, who is my refuge—then no harm will befall you, no disaster will come near your tent. For he will command his angels concerning you to guard you in all your ways. (Ps. 91:1–11)

According to David, the enemy would succumb to a superior force, ensuring the preservation of the twelve tribes—as was the scenario in 1991.

Five years later, Israel celebrated "Jerusalem 3000." The Old Testament record of what King David accomplished is found in First Chronicles chapter 16—which bears a striking resemblance to Psalm 96.

We'll begin with the record in Chronicles, and then move to the corresponding Psalm.

> Let the heavens rejoice, let the earth be glad; let them say among the nations, "The Lord reigns!" Let the sea resound, and all that is in it; let the fields be jubilant, and everything in them! Then the trees of the forest will sing, they will sing for joy before the Lord, for he comes to judge the earth. (1 Chr. 16:31–33)

> Let the heavens rejoice, let the earth be glad; let the sea resound, and all that is in it; let the fields be jubilant, and everything in them. Then all the trees of

> the forest will sing for joy; they will sing before the Lord, for he comes, he comes to judge the earth. He will judge the world in righteousness and the peoples in his truth. (Ps. 96:11–13)

David celebrated the Ark of the Covenant—not only in person, but also in his prophetic writings. His prophecy of the twelve tribes celebrating the Ark of the Covenant was written in Psalm 96—and it came to pass in 1996.

These sections of history and prophecy in the Old Testament are not only in alignment, but both prophesy of a future world where justice shall be made known to all by a righteous God.

We now move to the single most important moment of the twentieth century for the twelve tribes: Israel's statehood. Psalm 48 corresponds to that year, and corresponds to the Exodus period, when the twelve tribes would return to the Holy Land.

> Great is the Lord, and most worthy of praise, in the city of our God, his holy

mountain. It is beautiful in its loftiness, the joy of the whole earth. Like the utmost heights of Zaphon is Mount Zion, the city of the Great King. . . . As we have heard, so have we seen in the city of the Lord Almighty, in the city of our God: God makes her secure forever. *Selah* Within your temple, O God, we meditate on your unfailing love. Like your name, O God, your praise reaches to the ends of the earth; your right hand is filled with righteousness. Mount Zion rejoices, the villages of Judah are glad because of your judgments. Walk about Zion, go around her, count her towers, consider well her ramparts, view her citadels, that you may tell of them to the next generation. For this God is our God for ever and ever; he will be our guide even to the end. (Ps. 48:1, 2, 8–14)

In 1948, Jerusalem—the City of David—again became the home to those who follow Moses.[3] The "villages of Judah are glad," for the God of Israel gathered his people after they had been scattered for nearly 2000 years. The psalmist sings forth admiration for God, the city, and the land.

The first point about Psalm 48 to be examined in detail is the phrase, "beautiful in its loftiness." This descriptive statement emanates from a Hebrew term which means "branch of a tree."[4] This "tree" is the house of Israel—replanted—which had been cut off in the first century A.D.

A reference to Israel being broken off and replanted is found in the New Testament: "[T]hey [the twelve tribes] were broken off because of unbelief. . . . And if they do not persist in unbelief, they will be grafted in, for God is able to graft them in again" (Rom. 11:20, 23). This prophecy of Israel being "grafted in" (at a future point in time) corresponds to the replanting found in Psalm 48. The psalmist indicates that the tree of Israel would be replanted, and it is described as "beautiful."

To gain a sense of relevance with regard to how this "tree" applies to the fulfillment of prophecy and the timing of it, the second point to be examined in this Psalm involves the group of people who would correspond to God's prophecy: the "next generation." The significance of this particular "generation" is understood when viewed from the Hebrew language. The Hebrew word for "next" is *acharon*, which literally means the "last" generation.[5] Herein, the "last generation" of Psalm 48 is the one planted in 1948.

To grasp the magnitude of what this planting means for end-time events, we turn to another "prophet": Jesus Christ. When the Son of God prophesied of end-time events, he made a direct reference to the "last generation":

> Now learn this lesson from the fig tree: As soon as its twigs get tender and its leaves come out, you know that summer is near. Even so, when you see all these things, you know that it is near, right at the door. I tell you the truth, this generation will certainly not pass away

until all these things [end-time events] have happened. (Matt. 24:32–34)

The astounding connection to prophecy is as follows: the "last generation" spoken of by the psalmist 3000 years ago—which was planted like a "fig tree" in 1948—is "this generation" spoken of by Christ 2000 years ago. In essence, the prophecies made by the Son of God regarding his second coming, the Apocalypse, and the millennial kingdom shall be witnessed by the "last generation"—the one that began with the birth of Israel. Prophecy is marked in time. Consider Psalm 49:1–4:

> Hear this, all you peoples; listen, all who live in this world, both low and high, rich and poor alike: My mouth will speak words of wisdom; the utterance from my heart will give understanding. I will turn my ear to a proverb; with the harp I will expound my riddle.

From this Psalm, the following two points are evidently clear: there is a riddle in the Psalms, and it shall be revealed. Additionally, as this thought occurs in Psalm 49, it speaks to this riddle being disclosed at a point in time following the gathering of Israel.

Parallel to this thought are the writings of the prophet Daniel. He knew that his prophecies regarding end-time events would be "sealed until the time of the end" (Dan. 12:9), but he also knew that his prophecies would be unsealed when the time of the end entered humanity's stage. Therein, the "wise will understand" (Dan. 12:10).

Consider the words that David wrote in the 102nd Psalm: "Let this be written for a future generation, that a people not yet created may praise the Lord" (Ps. 102:18). One thousand years before the time of Christ, King David spoke to a "future generation"— in the *102nd* Psalm. Herein, the "future generation" of Psalm *102* would be upon the Earth in *2002*.

The Hebrew term for "future" generation is *acharon*—the same term used to describe the "last" generation of Psalm 48. Herein, both Psalm 48 and Psalm 102 refer to the "last generation," *the* one that shall witness prophetic fulfillment. (Logically speaking, if the prophetic words are to have any significance, then the generation of Psalm 102 must be informed—that they are in fact the generation spoken of by the author. Otherwise, the prophetic words would have little meaning.)

Psalm 102:13 reads: "You [God] will arise and have compassion on Zion, for it is time to show favor to her; the appointed time has come." These prophetic words specifically address divine intervention, which is set to engage at a defined moment in time—the time that corresponds to the "last generation."

Having reviewed the "future generation" of Psalm 102, we now turn our attention to the second part of the Psalm: the "people not yet created." Exactly whom was David referring to in his prophetic picture?

When the Psalms were written, the world was divided into two groups: the twelve tribes and the Gentiles. The Lord of Heaven had made a covenant with a man named Abraham (c. 2000 B.C.) and initiated the beginnings of the twelve tribes (which are named after the twelve sons of Jacob: Abraham's grandson). Twenty centuries after God's covenant with Abraham, the world witnessed the first coming of the Messiah. In his first coming, Christ was sent not only to "the lost sheep of Israel" (Matt. 15:24), but also was a "light for the Gentiles" (Isa. 42:6). It was following his presence that the "people" were created: the kingdom of Christ. The New Testament documents this addition—when it makes reference to the three groups of people that currently fill the Earth: "Jews . . . Gentiles . . . [and] the church of God [Christ's kingdom]" (1 Cor. 10:32 KJV).

With this understanding, Psalm 102 addresses the following: the "people not yet created" applies to the kingdom of Christ and the "future generation" applies to both Christ's kingdom and the "Jews"—the twelve tribes from which David was born.

(Note: For years, scholars questioned the existence of King David because there were no written records outside of the Bible documenting his reign in Jerusalem. However, in 1994, archaeologists discovered an inscription written upon a stone in Aramaic that refers to the "House of David." Found in the ancient city of Dan, the inscription dates to the ninth century B.C., and marks the first extrabiblical reference to David ever discovered.)

This King David not only spoke forth prophetic statements that relate to his heritage, but also prophesied of a time when an entirely new group of people would be upon the Earth. Additionally, as these two groups would be living side by side in the world, the time frame for fulfillment of prophecy would apply to both.

With regard to the timing of prophetic fulfillment, it is important to note the *symmetry of history*, as it applies to the twelve tribes and the kingdom of Christ: Twenty centuries were allotted to the twelve tribes (from Abraham to the first coming of Christ), and to date, twenty centuries have been allotted to the "people" created (from the first coming of Christ to the twenty-first century). If the first coming of the Messiah was fulfilled twenty centuries after the covenant was made with Abraham, then there is ample reason to conclude that the second coming of the Messiah shall be fulfilled twenty centuries after the start of the New Covenant—which adds further weight to the "future generation" of Psalm 102 being upon the Earth in 2002.

Now that we have established the composition and timing of the "last generation," the final question is: What exactly did David communicate? When he says let "this" be written for a "future generation," what did he refer to in his writings? Look at the last four verses of Psalm 102.

The Code of Psalms

> In the beginning you [God] laid the foundations of the earth, and the heavens are the work of your hands. They will perish, but you remain; they will all wear out like a garment. Like clothing you will change them and they will be discarded. But you remain the same, and your years will never end. The children of your servants will live in your presence; their descendants will be established before you.

This Earth has a finite life span. The future Earth is another dimension—where living in the presence of God is forever. When David wrote to the "last generation" in Psalm 102, he spoke to prophecies that shall come to pass—in *anticipation* of the future Earth.

To mark these prophecies, we now turn our attention to the heavens, which God designed to communicate knowledge to Earth. The prophets have revealed in their ancient writings that stars and planets function like a heavenly calendar marking time. In Psalm 19, David spoke of the diamonds that sparkle against the midnight sky and the knowledge that they communicate: "The heavens declare the glory of God; the skies proclaim the work of his hands. Day after day they pour forth speech; night after night they display knowledge" (Ps. 19:1, 2).

The arrangement of celestial bodies in the zodiac reveals Heaven's knowledge, marking earthly events with celestial statements. Although celestial displays can announce future events (such as the first coming of Christ), they can also announce the fulfillment of prophecy (such as the birth of God's Son).

The wise men knew to travel to the Holy Land in search of the Christ Child because they were informed by the arrangement of stars and planets. Jesus Christ himself gave the apostle John a vision of the celestial arrangement that marked his birth:

> A great and wondrous sign appeared in heaven: a woman [the constellation Virgo] clothed with the sun, with the moon under her feet and a crown of

twelve stars on her head. She [Israel (Mary)] was pregnant and cried out in pain as she was about to give birth [to the Christ Child]. (Rev. 12:1, 2)

The sun, shining through the constellation Virgo, was in alignment with the moon when Mary was about to give birth to Jesus. In this manner, the celestial clock heralded divine revelation. Additionally, according to divine prophecy, Heaven's celestial timepiece continues to roll forward, declaring knowledge.

With this vantage point in mind, we now move to the calendar years of 1999 and 2000, when the Earth witnessed two significant planetary conjunctions.

Firstly, on August 18, 1999, eight planets in our solar system formed the "Grand Cross." Thought to be one of the most significant astronomical alignments in nearly two thousand years, this configuration of planets literally formed a cross in the heavens. With the exception of Pluto, all of the planets were either "squared against" or "opposite" one another. By way of this planetary cross, Heaven "spoke" to Earth: THE "FOUR HORSEMEN OF THE APOCALYPSE" HAD BEEN RELEASED. This stunning announcement is found in Psalm 99: "Thou answeredst them, O Lord our God: thou wast a God that forgavest them, though thou tookest vengeance of their inventions [evil thoughts manifested]" (Ps. 99:8 KJV). Collectively, the "Four Horsemen of the Apocalypse" bring the righteousness of forgiveness, and the justice that delivers "vengeance."

Nine months after the "Grand Cross," the Earth witnessed its second, remarkable astronomical occurrence: the "Grand Alignment." On May 5, 2000, the Earth, the sun, and the moon were in alignment with Mercury, Venus, Mars, Saturn, and Jupiter. This planetary alignment marked Heaven's celestial exclamation point: THE FIFTH SEAL HAD BEEN OPENED. THE MARTYRS HAD BEEN RELEASED. This spectacular spiritual event is marked in Psalm 100: "Enter his gates with thanksgiving and his courts with praise; give thanks to him and praise his name" (Ps. 100:4).

Those who "enter his gates" into the "courts" of Heaven are the martyrs.

With this part of the prophetic puzzle now complete, our world stands before a divine threshold: the second coming of Jesus Christ. (Interestingly, the "Grand Alignment" has been identified with the 2 B.C. conjunction of planets known as the "Christmas Star." As recorded in the book of Matthew, this "star" heralded the *first* coming of Christ.)

With this dramatic backdrop of celestial announcements, world events, and prophetic statements, we now turn our attention to the prophecies that pertain to end-time events: Christ's second coming to gather the kingdom, the Apocalypse, and the establishment of the millennial kingdom.

We return to the prophetic words of David, where in Psalm 102, he spoke of divine intervention: "[T]he Lord will rebuild Zion and appear in his glory" (Ps. 102:16). David prophesied that the Lord would "appear in his glory," and that it would come to pass during the "last generation."

Now, we turn to the prophetic picture painted by Christ—when he spoke of his second coming to Earth: his appearance in "glory."

> [T]he sun will be darkened, and the moon will not give its light; the stars will fall from the sky, and the heavenly bodies will be shaken. At that time men will see the Son of Man coming in clouds with great power and glory. And he will send his angels and gather his elect from the four winds, from the ends of the earth to the ends of the heavens. (Mark 13:24–27)

When God turns out the light, Christ will return with his angels for his kingdom, and gather "his elect" from the "four winds." Exactly what are the four winds? The psalmist referred to them when he prophesied of the "gathering" in Psalm 107.

> Give thanks to the Lord, for he is good; his love endures forever. Let the redeemed of the Lord say this—those he redeemed from the hand of the foe,

those he gathered from the lands, from east and west, from north and south. (Ps. 107:1–3)

The four winds are from the "east and west, from north and south." This prophetic statement is placed in Psalm 107, for it marks the second coming of Christ to redeem his elect—IN CALENDAR YEAR 2007!

To anchor this thought, we turn back to the words of Psalm 106: "Save us, O Lord our God, and gather us from the nations, that we may give thanks to your holy name and glory in your praise" (Ps. 106:47). This is the collective voice of the kingdom of Christ—in anticipation of the second coming.

(Note: When Jesus Christ prophesied of this future time, he stated that no one would know the specific *moment* in time—the *"day or hour"*—when he would return: "No one knows about that day or hour, not even the angels in heaven, nor the Son, but only the Father" (Matt. 24:36). The "year" was not included in Christ's prophecy because mankind would know the year—the psalmist had already recorded that prophetic statement in his writings.)

Following Christ's return for his kingdom, the seventh seal will open, and wrath shall commence. Then the final chapter of Gabriel's prophecy—given centuries before the time of Christ—shall come to pass. Psalms 105 and 107 prophesy of this scenario.

> He sent darkness and made the land dark—for had they not rebelled against his words? He turned their waters into blood, causing their fish to die. Their land teemed with frogs, which went up into the bedrooms of their rulers. He spoke, and there came swarms of flies, and gnats throughout their country. He turned their rain into hail, with lightning throughout their land; he struck down their vines and fig trees and shattered the trees of their country. He spoke, and the locusts came, grasshoppers without number; they ate up every green

thing in their land, ate up the produce of their soil. (Ps. 105:28–35)

He [God] turned rivers into a desert, flowing springs into thirsty ground, and fruitful land into a salt waste, because of the wickedness of those who lived there. (Ps. 107:33, 34)

Psalm 105 references the plagues that befell Egypt—which have an eerie parallel to the plagues of the seventh seal as revealed in the Book of Revelation. Psalm 107 references global calamities, which mark the start date of the seventieth "seven": 2007. It is then that the two prophets of God shall stop the rain, turning "rivers into a desert."

During the time of the final seven years, there will be two groups of people left on the planet: the twelve tribes and the Gentiles. During this time, the twelve tribes shall cry unto their God: "Give us aid against the enemy, for the help of man is worthless. With God we will gain the victory, and he will trample down our enemies" (Ps. 108:12, 13). During the final chapter of Gabriel's prophecy, the strength of flesh and blood will matter little, as spiritual power will overpower the planet. The twelve tribes shall cry unto their God for "victory"—over spiritual darkness.

Psalm 109 prophesies of *consummate* darkness: the Antichrist—and the condemnation that shall be upon him.

> Set thou a wicked man over him: and let Satan stand at his right hand. (Ps. 109:6 KJV)

> When he is tried, let him be found guilty, and may his prayers condemn him. May his days be few; may another take his place of leadership. May his children be fatherless and his wife a widow. May his children be wandering beggars; may they be driven from their ruined homes. May a creditor seize all he has; may strangers plunder the fruits of his labor. May no one extend kind-

ness to him or take pity on his fatherless children. May his descendants be cut off, their names blotted out from the next [following] generation.[6] May the iniquity of his fathers be remembered before the Lord; may the sin of his mother never be blotted out. May their sins always remain before the Lord, that he may cut off the memory of them from the earth. For he never thought of doing a kindness, but hounded to death the poor and the needy and the brokenhearted. He loved to pronounce a curse—may it come on him; he found no pleasure in blessing—may it be far from him. He wore cursing as his garment; it entered into his body like water, into his bones like oil. May it be like a cloak wrapped about him, like a belt tied forever around him. (Ps. 109:7–19)

Although the identity of the beast shall remain sealed until the time of the seventh seal, divine prophecy states that he is the "eighth king," and that he "belongs to [is of] the seven [seventh king]" (Rev. 17:11). Herein, we know that the Antichrist is in a lineage of worldly power, which finds its roots in a dark spiritual heritage.

By way of his beast, Satan will wage war against Heaven, seeking to eliminate man from the Earth. "For then there will be great distress, unequaled from the beginning of the world until now—and never to be equaled again" (Matt. 24:21). Without fearsome divine intervention, "no one would survive" (Matt. 24:22).

At the midpoint of Gabriel's seventieth "seven," the Antichrist will rise to assume his throne—only to be destroyed by Christ's Apocalypse. Psalm 110 prophesies of it.

> The Lord says to my Lord: "Sit at my right hand until I make your enemies a footstool for your feet." The Lord will extend your mighty scepter from Zion; you will rule in the midst of your enemies. Your troops will be willing on your day of battle. Arrayed in holy majesty, from the womb of the dawn you will receive the dew of your

youth. The Lord has sworn and will not change his mind: "You are a priest forever, in the order of Melchizedek." The Lord is at your right hand; he will crush kings on the day of his wrath. He will judge the nations, heaping up the dead and crushing the rulers of the whole earth. (Ps. 110:1–6)

"Your troops will be willing on your day of battle [against the kings]." The battle is Armageddon, the "kings" are the "ten kings" who give their power to the Antichrist (Rev. 17:12, 13), and the troops are the angels—which include the "elect" gathered by Christ in 2007: "his called, chosen and faithful followers" (Rev. 17:14). The souls who are transformed *by* the Messiah shall descend out of Heaven *with* the Messiah to bring an end to the Antichrist.

This prophecy of Psalm 110 is fulfilled in Psalm 114; it opens with a reference to God delivering the Israelites out of Egypt, and a statement about divine intervention during the exodus.

> When Israel came out of Egypt, the house of Jacob from a people of foreign tongue, Judah became God's sanctuary, Israel his dominion. The sea looked and fled, the Jordan turned back. (Ps. 114:1–3)

The parallel train of thought is unmistakable: Just as the will of Heaven overpowered the Egyptian Pharaoh, so shall it again with the Antichrist.

In the year 2014, divine intervention shall bring an end to Satan's dominion over the Earth—this place will *"tremble"* when Christ descends out of Heaven with his armies: "Tremble, O earth, at the presence of the Lord, at the presence of the God of Jacob" (Ps. 114:7).

The "God of Jacob" shall again deliver the twelve tribes—into a land that overflows with the presence of Heaven. He is the God, "who turned the rock into a pool, the hard rock into springs of water" (Ps. 114:8).

As the Lord God worked miracles in the desert by making water to flow where there was none, and blessed the Israelites in their journey to the Promised Land, so shall he again work miracles by giving them a thousand-year kingdom—and Christ as their King. In the year 2015, the glorified Christ will reign as King of kings and Lord of lords—and the twelve tribes shall rejoice! Psalm 115 marks the glory of it.

> Not to us, O Lord, not to us but to your name be the glory, because of your love and faithfulness. . . . O house of Israel, trust in the Lord—he is their help and shield. O house of Aaron, trust in the Lord—he is their help and shield. You who fear him, trust in the Lord—he is their help and shield. The Lord remembers us and will bless us: He will bless the house of Israel, he will bless the house of Aaron, he will bless those who fear the Lord—small and great alike. May the Lord make you increase, both you and your children. May you be blessed by the Lord, the Maker of heaven and earth. The highest heavens belong to the Lord, but the earth he has given to man. It is not the dead who

> praise the Lord, those who go down to silence; it is we who extol the Lord, both now and forevermore. Praise the Lord. (Ps. 115:1, 9–18)

Without question, these Psalms bear an unmistakable resemblance to what is now recorded in the history books and what shall be. Recognizing the harmony that flows through historical, celestial, and prophetic pictures, the obvious question arises: What kind of supernatural intelligence is this? This is a God that has unerring foreknowledge of future events—which cannot be fathomed by human intellect—and has communicated those prophecies in the book called the Bible.

This book is astonishing in its presentation, for the words contained within are Heaven's "symphony" to Earth: "All Scripture is God-breathed" (2 Tim. 3:16). This eternal intelligence breathed forth words of light to the prophets, and they in turn wrote what was given. "For prophecy never had its origin in the will of man, but men spoke from God as they were carried along by the

Holy Spirit" (2 Peter 1:21). The biblical texts emanate from this God communicating divine revelation via Spirit.

Only the hand of supernatural intelligence could bring forth a literary design that weaves life, history, and prophecy into a coherent, unbreakable pattern that spans sixty-six books, and has stood for thousands of years. In this "last generation," looking back on this production, we can only be awestruck, as we are now on the verge of crossing into the fulfillment of divine prophecy. Armed with this understanding, the cry of the righteous is unmistakable, for it is the cry of God: "[M]ay sinners vanish from the earth and the wicked be no more" (Ps. 104:35).

Act Two

Act Two

5

THE DOORS OF PARADISE

Here I am! I stand at the door and knock. If anyone hears my voice and opens the door, I will come in and eat with him, and he with me.

—The Son of God (Rev. 3:20)

The right to live on the other side emanates from a gift, for the doors of paradise are opened when darkness is overcome and the light is embraced. When the soul is illuminated by words of truth, it is rescued from death. In a moment of time, the finite becomes infinite.

When the door of the heart is opened to the Son of God, divine energy pours forth, filling the soul, sealing it for eternity. By way of Spirit created within, a soul is born into the kingdom of Christ, forever a son of the Father. Therein, that soul shall live to see paradise.

> He who has an ear, let him hear what the Spirit says to the churches. To him who overcomes, I [Christ] will give the right to eat from the tree of life, which is in the paradise of God. (Rev. 2:7)

To "overcome" is to embrace God's grace, which is his unmerited divine favor. This divine favor is a gift from Heaven delivered by the Messiah. Those who embrace him enter his kingdom in this world and shall enter the paradise of God on the next Earth. There, with access to the tree of life, the rescued souls shall have an everlasting place in the very life-giving presence of God.

This new agreement from Heaven was demonstrated during the Crucifixion, when the Son of God promised paradise to a man condemned to death. The crucified man recognized that Jesus was the Messiah and said, "'Jesus, remember me when you come into your kingdom.' Jesus answered him, 'I tell you the truth, today you will be with me in paradise'" (Luke 23:42, 43).

The Messiah justified a condemned man (acquitting him of all sin). In an instant, the *condemned* soul became the *saved* soul. On the Cross, condemnation was removed and replaced with God's righteousness. This was the New Covenant Jesus brought from the Father: eternal life would now be granted by the grace of Heaven. The words of Jesus yielded a guarantee of life everlasting in the future world.[1]

Christ was able to grant paradise to a man with a criminal record because the Messiah's blood was the ransom paid by God to release souls condemned to die: "[T]he Son of Man did not come to be served, but to serve, and to give his life as a ransom for many" (Mark 10:45). When the blood of Christ is given in exchange for the life of a soul, that soul is liberated from mortality. To "overcome" in this life is to accept the ransom that God has already given.

As recorded by the apostle Peter: "[Y]ou know that it was not with perishable things such as silver or gold that you were redeemed from the empty way of life . . . but with the precious blood of Christ, a lamb without blemish or defect. He was chosen before the creation of the world, but was revealed in these last times for your sake" (1 Peter 1:18–20).

Christ is the *full* payment for souls to cross the spiritual divide. Man cannot earn his freedom; the cleansing of sin is without charge. If any payment from mankind is necessary to attain salvation, then the blood of Christ was an insufficient ransom. Through his Son, the heavenly Father "rescued us from the dominion of darkness and brought us into the kingdom of the Son he loves"

(Col. 1:13). God established the New Covenant, whereby the kingdom of Christ would be upon Earth, filled with souls who accept Heaven's gift.

Once in the kingdom, the liberated soul is sanctified—set apart—for all eternity. No power of darkness can alter the fate of a soul reserved by the heavenly Father. "I tell you the truth, whoever hears my word and believes him who sent me has eternal life and will not be condemned; he has crossed over from death to life" (John 5:24).

According to Christ's prophecy, once a soul crosses into eternal life, there is no slipping back. If eternal life is granted, it cannot be revoked. Instantaneously, the power of death over the soul is overcome. The condemned man who hung on the cross did not evolve into a state of righteousness; he was made to be that way. That's why he could be guaranteed paradise—Jesus apportioned grace on the Cross.

The apostle Paul—appointed by Heaven to bring Christ's gospel to the world—wrote of this divine favor given by God: "For it is by grace you have been saved, through faith—and this is not from yourselves, it is the gift of God—not by works, so that no one can boast" (Eph. 2:8, 9). "And if [salvation is] by grace, then it is no longer by works; if it were, grace would no longer be grace" (Rom. 11:6). Grace is no longer grace if the hand of man is necessary to push his own soul across the spiritual divide. It is through an act of God that immortality is attained. Through his love God gave us a redeemer:

> [W]hen the kindness and love of God our Savior appeared, he saved us, not because of righteous things we had done, but because of his mercy. He saved us through the washing of rebirth and renewal by the Holy Spirit, whom he poured out on us generously through Jesus Christ our Savior. (Titus 3:4–6)

> [Y]ou were washed, you were sanctified, you were justified in the name of the Lord Jesus Christ and by the Spirit of our God. (1 Cor. 6:11)

It is not because of individual righteous acts that a soul is washed with living water from Heaven. The Son of God *brought* the kingdom of God—a spiritual kingdom where entrance would not be earned, but granted. The Creator extended *his* hand to Earth—through his Son—so that he could pour out his Spirit generously.

Christ himself elaborated upon the spiritual nature of his kingdom, "The kingdom of God does not come with your careful observation, . . . because the kingdom of God is within you" (Luke 17:20, 21). "For the kingdom of God is not a matter of eating and drinking, but of righteousness, peace and joy in the Holy Spirit" (Rom. 14:17). The true kingdom of God is not about carnal regulations that legislate food and drink; it is about the Holy Spirit's spiritual presence and nature dwelling within the believer.

God is upon Earth by those who are born of his nature. In this manner, the prophecy spoken before the time of Christ is fulfilled: "I will live with them and walk among them, and I will be their God, and they will be my people" (2 Cor. 6:16). This reference to Old Testament prophecy is how the apostle Paul explained that God would dwell with his people—by way of Christ. In his writings, Paul explained the magnitude of this God by describing him as "the blessed and only Ruler, the King of kings and Lord of lords, who alone is immortal and who lives in unapproachable light, whom no one has seen or can see" (1 Tim. 6:15, 16).

The apostle provided an intriguing picture of the supernatural intelligence that orchestrated the defeat of Satan and the rescue of souls from the planet. This victory—achieved by God—is given to souls upon Earth through Christ's gospel.

The true nature of this God—fully declared through Jesus—was first disclosed hundreds of years earlier by Moses, for he revealed the heart of this omnipotent intelligence: "The Lord, the Lord, the compassionate and gracious God, slow to anger, abounding in love and faithfulness, maintaining love to thousands, and forgiving wickedness, rebellion and sin" (Exod. 34:6, 7).

The Doors of Paradise 197

When Moses first wrote these words, he looked forward to the day that God would send a redeemer. He knew that through the coming Messiah, the heavenly Father would fully extend this compassion to Earth. However, neither Moses nor any other Old Testament prophet knew that one day, all bloodlines could be born of Spirit saved into the kingdom of Christ.

In the Holy Land, Jesus expounded upon this New Covenant from Heaven, explaining how to see the kingdom:

> Now there was a man of the Pharisees named Nicodemus, a member of the Jewish ruling council. He came to Jesus at night and said, "Rabbi, we know you are a teacher who has come from God. For no one could perform the miraculous signs you are doing if God were not with him."
>
> In reply Jesus declared, "I tell you the truth, no one can see the kingdom of God unless he is born again."
>
> "How can a man be born when he is old?" Nicodemus asked. "Surely he can-

> not enter a second time into his mother's womb to be born!"
>
> Jesus answered, "I tell you the truth, no one can enter the kingdom of God unless he is born of water and the Spirit. Flesh gives birth to flesh, but the Spirit gives birth to spirit.
>
> "You should not be surprised at my saying, 'You must be born again.'" (John 3:1–7)

The flesh of man gives birth to the flesh of man. In contrast, God gives birth to an eternal, invisible, spiritual seed within the soul of man. This is the second birth of which Jesus and his apostles spoke. As recorded in the writings of Peter: "[Y]ou have been born again, not of perishable seed, but of imperishable, through the living and enduring word of God" (1 Peter 1:23). When the "living and enduring word of God" is believed, then the Creator creates seed within the soul that cannot perish.

This spiritual seed—which gives birth to eternal life—is "Christ in you, the hope of glory" (Col. 1:27). The Spirit of "Christ in you" is both "life" in this world and the hope of future "glory" in the next. When the Spirit of Christ lives within, the soul life of that person will live again in a spiritual body.

No act of man can cause the spiritual seed of Christ to be removed or destroyed. "The new birth is a decisive, unrepeatable, and irrevocable act of God."[2] The soul that is born again of Spirit cannot be unborn. The indwelling Spirit is Heaven's spiritual seal upon the soul, reserving it for all eternity.

> Having believed, you were marked in him with a seal, the promised Holy Spirit, who is a deposit guaranteeing our inheritance until the redemption of those who are God's possession—to the praise of his glory. (Eph. 1:13, 14)

The promised Spirit of Christ "marks" and "seals" the soul, "guaranteeing" a heavenly "inheritance." No dark power can break the seal that Heaven places upon a saved soul. The Spirit of Christ—living within—is

Heaven's "deposit." It is God's down payment within his "possession," which will be redeemed when the Son of God returns with his angels. In the words of the apostle John, "Beloved, now are we the sons of God, and it doth not yet appear what we shall be: but we know that, when he shall appear, we shall be like him; for we shall see him as he is" (1 John 3:2 KJV).

In this life—right now—those souls who are born of the Holy Spirit are the sons of God. Although the next world has not been fully revealed, what has been revealed is that divine glory shall be unveiled in the clouds at the second coming of Christ. The Son of God will be seen in his glorified form, and those who ascend in the air shall be like him. This is the hope of glory.

What gives birth to this phenomenon is the spiritual seed of Christ within. That seed also gives birth to an inner transformation in this world. "For God hath not given us the spirit of fear; but of power, and of love, and of a sound mind" (2 Tim. 1:7 KJV). The

Spirit that God gives yields inner power and love. It displaces fear.

This is the catalyst to ignite the inner transformation that Paul described: "[I]f the Spirit of him who raised Jesus from the dead is living in you, he who raised Christ from the dead will also give life to your mortal bodies through his Spirit, who lives in you" (Rom. 8:11). When the Spirit that raised Jesus from the dead lives within, spiritual energy gives "life" to the mortal body. This is the renewal, the rebirth, caused by the introduction of divine energy from above.

The very attributes of God fill flesh and blood. The Spirit of Christ within is God's very essence; it is his "divine nature" (2 Peter 1:4). "God has poured out his love into our hearts by the Holy Spirit" (Rom. 5:5), and nothing can "separate us from the love of God that is in Christ Jesus our Lord" (Rom. 8:39). From before the foundation of this world, God planned to give Earth this grace:

> This grace was given us in Christ Jesus before the beginning of time, but it has now been revealed through the appearing of our Savior, Christ Jesus, who has destroyed death and has brought life and immortality to light through the gospel. (2 Tim. 1:9, 10)

"Life" and "immortality" are brought to light by Christ's gospel—his words. He enters the heart—by way of the second birth—when the door is opened to him:

> [I]f you confess with your mouth, "Jesus is Lord," and believe in your heart that God raised him from the dead, you will be saved. For it is with your heart that you believe and are justified, and it is with your mouth that you confess and are saved. (Rom. 10:9, 10)

When the Son of God is made to be your own Lord, your own soul crosses into eternal life. This confession of the heart produces the spiritual birth that overcomes spiritual darkness and yields a place in Christ's spiritual kingdom.

> [F]or everyone born of God overcomes the world. This is the victory that has overcome the world, even our faith. Who is it that overcomes the world? Only he who believes that Jesus is the Son of God. (1 John 5:4, 5)

This is Christ's gospel of faith, righteousness, and immortality. It is in sharp contrast to the Old Testament, where good works earned righteousness (Deut. 6:25).

This is why the focal point of all human history is Jesus Christ. He declared that mankind had crossed a threshold in the first century. That's why he told Nicodemus about the second birth. Moses didn't come to bring the spiritual birth—Jesus did.

By way of Jesus, the kingdom of God on Earth had finally dawned. The Messiah declared that he marked the start of a New Covenant from Heaven: "The Law [of Moses] and the Prophets [of the Old Testament] were proclaimed until John [the Baptist]. Since that time, the good news of the kingdom of God is being preached" (Luke 16:16).

Jesus justified the condemned man on the Cross not by the law of works but by the law of love. The Messiah brought faith, and that faith yielded justification. The Son of God did not come to Earth to reaffirm the Old Testament Law but to elevate the standard to that of love and grace: "Jesus [is] the mediator of a new covenant" (Heb. 12:24).

Christ's faith voided the Mosaic agreement. He "canceled the written code [the Law], with its regulations, that was against us and that stood opposed to us; he took it away, nailing it to the cross" (Col. 2:14). "Christ is the end of the law so that there may be righteousness for everyone who believes" (Rom. 10:4).

Although the Old Testament Law was perfect in its standard, it was "opposed" to man because it could not change the sin nature that Adam had passed on to him. No one could fulfill it completely because man is imperfect. This is why the people of the

Old Testament period sacrificed animals—to cover their sins.

With the New Covenant, however, there is no further need to make such sacrifices because Jesus was the Lamb given by God to cleanse sins—yielding "righteousness for everyone who believes."[3] Righteousness comes by faith in the sufficiency of that sacrifice. "For in the gospel a righteousness from God is revealed, a righteousness that is by faith . . . just as it is written: 'The righteous will live by faith'" (Rom. 1:17). This prophecy was fulfilled in Christ. All who open the door to him receive the "measure of faith" (Rom. 12:3) and "righteousness . . . by faith" (Phil. 3:9).

On the Cross, Christ took upon himself all that the world is (sinful), so that souls could become all that he is (righteous): "God made him who had no sin to be sin for us, so that in him we might become the righteousness of God" (2 Cor. 5:21). Righteousness yields the ability to stand before God without any sense of sin, guilt, or condemnation, completely worthy to be in the Almighty's presence.

This is what the Son of God came to give to mankind—the divine presence of God within forever. This is Christ's prophecy: "My sheep listen to my voice; I know them, and they follow me. I give them eternal life, and they shall never perish; no one can snatch them out of my hand. My Father, who has given them to me, is greater than all; no one can snatch them out of my Father's hand" (John 10:27–29).

6

THE DIVINE SIGN

And these signs will accompany those who believe: . . . they will speak in new tongues.

—The Son of God (Mark 16:17)

What separates Jesus Christ from every other "prophet" is that he rose from the dead and ascended into the heavens. Although some people render this divine revelation to be a "story," those who embrace the Son of God know it to be true. Heaven has given Earth a supernatural sign that Jesus *is* Earth's Messiah. Through the indwelling Spirit of Christ, a son of God is empowered to bring forth the divine sign: speaking in tongues. It is the sign of Christ—the indisputable proof of his Resurrection from the dead and of God's indwelling presence. It is the individual expression of faith, which declares that the Son ascended to the right hand of the Father.

Christ's sign of speaking in tongues is not spoken from the mind but is given by divine inspiration. Both angelic and human, the new languages are known by God but not by the one speaking. Therein, speaking in divinely inspired tongues is a supernatural manifestation; it is the irrefutable statement from Heaven that the one speaking has entered the kingdom of Christ and shall live to see the new Earth.

The writings of the apostle Peter demonstrate the magnitude of Christ's sign by

The Divine Sign

comparing it to Christ's transfiguration. After Jesus led Peter, James, and John to the top of a mountain, Jesus was transfigured before their eyes. He exuded divine light, and the apostles heard the audible voice of God.

> After six days Jesus took with him Peter, James and John the brother of James, and led them up a high mountain by themselves. There he was transfigured before them. His face shone like the sun, and his clothes became as white as the light. Just then there appeared before them Moses and Elijah, talking with Jesus.
>
> Peter said to Jesus, "Lord, it is good for us to be here. If you wish, I will put up three shelters—one for you, one for Moses and one for Elijah."
>
> While he was still speaking, a bright cloud enveloped them, and a voice from the cloud said, "This is my Son, whom I love; with him I am well pleased. Listen to him!"
>
> When the disciples heard this, they fell facedown to the ground, terrified. But Jesus came and touched them. "Get

up," he said. "Don't be afraid." When they looked up, they saw no one except Jesus. (Matt. 17:1–8)

Unquestionably, Peter, John, and James underwent a serious alteration in their thinking. The mind-set they had walking up the mountain was not the same as they had going back down the mountain. Imagine hearing God and seeing Christ transfigured. Yet Peter said that Heaven's divine presence was made even "more sure" by the audible voice of new tongues. According to the apostle, Christ's supernatural sign of tongues exceeded in magnitude the supernatural sign witnessed on the mountaintop that day. In his second letter, the apostle addressed this incredible subject of the divine sign:

> Simon Peter, a servant and apostle of Jesus Christ, To those who through the righteousness of our God and Savior Jesus Christ have received a faith as precious as ours: Grace and peace be yours in abundance through the knowl-

edge of God and of Jesus our Lord. (2 Peter 1:1, 2)

> [W]e have not followed cunningly devised fables, when we made known unto you the power and coming of our Lord Jesus Christ, but were eyewitnesses of his majesty. For he received from God the Father honour and glory, when there came such a voice to him from the excellent glory, This is my beloved Son, in whom I am well pleased. And this voice which came from heaven we heard, when we were with him in the holy mount. We have also a more sure word of prophecy; whereunto ye do well that ye take heed, as unto a light that shineth in a dark place, until the day dawn, and the day star arise in your hearts. (2 Peter 1:16–19 KJV)

In his writings, Peter described Christ's sign of tongues as a "more sure word of [divine] prophecy." He had something more conclusive than what he saw and heard on the mountaintop—the voice of God within. Peter manifested the indwelling Spirit of Christ and spoke divine prophecy by way of new languages.

The apostle exhorted the kingdom of Christ to "heed" this sign of Christ. According to Peter, by speaking in tongues, the kingdom of Christ brings forth the light of the day star—the divine light that shines in spiritual darkness. The prophecy spoken by Peter states that this illumination upon Earth will continue until the second coming of Christ, when he returns to gather his kingdom. When that "day dawns," the sign of the Resurrection will cease because Christ will be seen "face to face" (1 Cor. 13:12). When the rescued souls meet their Lord in the air, the light of the day star will exit the planet.

After the second coming of Christ, no one will be left on Earth to speak in tongues. At that time, when the sign ends, the future of mankind will undergo a dramatic change, just as history did when the sign first began two millenniums ago.

The Divine Sign 213

The history of mankind witnessed dramatic divine intervention in the first century, and man's future was forever altered. Once the light of the day star dawned on the planet, nothing could stop its illumination.

Peter and the other eleven apostles were the first among Christ's followers to speak forth the divine light of "tongues." The Twelve Apostles first spoke in tongues on the holy day of Pentecost, which was ten days after Christ's ascension and fifty days after his Resurrection. On that day, man's great high priest—Jesus Christ—baptized his apostles with the Holy Spirit.

On the very day of Christ's Resurrection, he spoke of this holy day. When he appeared before Peter and the other disciples, he first showed them the physical signs of his Crucifixion—proving that he was nailed to the Cross and resurrected. In addition, he prophesied that his disciples would soon bring forth the supernatural sign of his Resurrection.

> On the evening of that first day of the week [Sunday, in biblical times], when the disciples were together, with the doors locked for fear of the Jews, Jesus came and stood among them and said, "Peace be with you!" After he said this, he showed them his hands and side. The disciples were overjoyed when they saw the Lord. Again Jesus said, "Peace be with you! As the Father has sent me, I am sending you." And with that he breathed on them and said, "Receive the Holy Spirit." (John 20:19–22)

On Resurrection Sunday, the risen Messiah spoke forth prophecy; he foretold that his followers would receive into manifestation the Holy Spirit by way of speaking in tongues.[1] By "breathing" on the disciples, the Son of God demonstrated how to manifest the sign. The apostles understood that by the human act of speech—carried along by breathing—they would speak forth new languages.

The Divine Sign

From Resurrection Sunday until the day of the ascension, the risen Messiah prepared his apostles for Pentecost. As this holy day approached, the Lord told his disciples:

> Do not leave Jerusalem, but wait for the gift my Father promised, which you have heard me speak about. For John baptized with water, but in a few days you will be baptized with the Holy Spirit. . . . [Y]ou will receive power when the Holy Spirit comes on you; and you will be my witnesses in Jerusalem, and in all Judea and Samaria, and to the ends of the earth. (Acts 1:4, 5, 8)

> "I am going to send you what my Father has promised; but stay in the city until you have been clothed with power from on high."

When he had led them out to the vicinity of Bethany, he lifted up his hands and blessed them. While he was blessing them, he left them and was taken up into heaven. Then they worshiped him and returned to Jerusalem with great joy.

> And they stayed continually at the temple, praising God. (Luke 24:49–53)

As Christ lifted off to the clouds, the apostles stood staring into the heavens with the assurance that their Lord would fulfill his promise. Then, the apostles stayed "continually at the temple" because that's where man's great high priest would clothe the Twelve with "power from on high."

After Christ ascended, Peter prepared for the fulfillment of Christ's prophecy. This included selecting a new apostle—Matthias—to replace Judas Iscariot. Peter declared to a multitude of faithful followers (about 120 people), that Matthias would become a witness of the Resurrection with him and the other apostles. On the eve of Pentecost, Peter addressed the followers of Jesus:

> "[I]t is necessary to choose one of the men who have been with us the whole time the Lord Jesus went in and out among us, beginning from John's baptism to the time when Jesus was

taken up from us. For one of these must become a witness with us of his resurrection." . . . Then they cast lots, and the lot fell to Matthias; so he was added to the eleven apostles.

When the day of Pentecost came, they [the now Twelve Apostles] were all together in one place. Suddenly a sound like the blowing of a violent wind came from heaven and filled the whole house where they were sitting. They saw what seemed to be tongues of fire that separated and came to rest on each of them. All of them were filled with the Holy Spirit and began to speak in other tongues as the Spirit enabled them. (Acts 1:21, 22, 26; 2:1–4)

The spiritual shock of all ages burst upon the house of prayer during an hour of prayer. As powerful winds rushed throughout the corridors, flaming tongues of fire burned above the twelve men. With the visual sign of tongues given, the Twelve Apostles spoke forth new languages—becoming witnesses of the Resurrection by the sign of the Resurrection.

As caravans of devout followers of Moses traveled from many countries making their pilgrimage to Jerusalem, they had no idea what awaited them on Pentecost. As thousands of people gathered in quiet adoration to pray at the temple, heavenly signs shattered the silence. At 9:00 in the morning, God sent an unmistakable exclamation mark shooting through the hearts of the worshipers present: the prophecies of the Old Testament regarding the first coming of Christ had been fulfilled completely.

This demonstration of spiritual power culminated in God speaking to the "world" by way of the Twelve. Inspired by the Spirit of Christ within, the men from Galilee spoke multiple "foreign" languages, and people from many nations heard "God" speak. Thousands of people heard the wonderful works of God spoken in their ears in their native languages. By way of "new tongues" God announced the fulfillment of prophecy, testifying that Jesus was the Christ.

The Divine Sign 219

Pentecost was the unmistakable line of demarcation, separating the Law from faith. No longer would righteousness be earned; rather, it would be granted by the faith of Christ. This outpouring of the Spirit established the New Covenant with mankind: the kingdom of God would now live within flesh and blood, and it would be made known by the divine sign.

The indwelling Spirit of Christ "enabled" the Twelve to speak in new languages, but it was the apostles *themselves* who actually spoke the sign of Christ into being. The Spirit of Christ did not control them. The Twelve Apostles were in control of the Spirit. As explained by the apostle Paul: "The spirits of prophets are subject to the control of prophets" (1 Cor. 14:32). After Christ filled the Twelve with his Spirit, the apostles "breathed" (and spoke) the sign into evidence.

This mystifying display of supernatural energy in the temple caused the onlookers to be struck with disbelief:

Now there were staying in Jerusalem God-fearing Jews from every nation under heaven. When they heard this sound [of tongues], a crowd came together in bewilderment, because each one heard them speaking in his own language. Utterly amazed, they asked: "Are not all these men who are speaking Galileans? Then how is it that each of us hears them in his own native language? . . . [W]e hear them declaring the wonders of God in our own tongues!" Amazed and perplexed, they asked one another, "What does this mean?" Some, however, made fun of them and said, "They have had too much wine."

Then Peter stood up with the Eleven, raised his voice and addressed the crowd: "Fellow Jews and all of you who live in Jerusalem, let me explain this to you; listen carefully to what I say. These men are not drunk, as you suppose. It's only nine in the morning! No, this is what was spoken by the prophet Joel:

> "'In the last days, God says, I will pour out my Spirit on all people.'" (Acts 2:5–8, 11–17)

In order to establish the significance of what the crowd witnessed, Peter referred to Joel, one of the Old Testament prophets. Peter told the crowd that they had heard divine prophecy fulfilled in their ears.

Hundreds of years before Christ, Joel foretold of the day God would pour out his Spirit upon flesh and blood. Joel recorded the very words spoken by the Almighty: "I will pour out my Spirit on all people. . . . Even on my servants, both men and women, I will pour out my Spirit in those days" (Joel 2:28, 29). On Pentecost this prophecy came to pass.

This holy day represented fulfillment of not only Joel's prophecy but that of Isaiah as well: "[W]ith foreign lips and strange tongues God will speak to this people, to whom he said, 'This is the resting place, let the weary rest'; and, 'This is the place of repose'—but they would not listen" (Isa. 28:11, 12).

God said that he would speak to his people with "foreign lips" and "strange tongues." (The tongues are termed "strange" because they are not spoken on Earth but by angels, and "foreign" because they are unknown to the one speaking.) On Pentecost, this prophecy of new languages was fulfilled. Thereby, God brought souls into the kingdom of Christ, and within it, brought them to a place of confidence ("repose").

Yet for all of this, Isaiah foretold that there would be followers of Moses who would not embrace even a supernatural sign from God. On Pentecost, some devout followers of the Old Covenant even accused Peter of being drunk when he spoke in tongues.

Peter shrugged off the accusations and took center stage as he stood up to address the crowd. All eyes were riveted on Peter as he began to teach about Jesus Christ and eternal life. Without hesitation, he set in order the things pertaining to this Jesus of Nazareth

The Divine Sign

and the New Covenant that he had established on Earth. The result of this great oration was the acceptance of the covenant by thousands of people on that one day.

Interestingly, just fifty days earlier, this same Peter had been hiding behind locked doors in fear for his own life. Peter had even denied knowing the Lord; he had nothing to say publicly concerning him. With the Crucifixion of Jesus, Peter and the others had been overcome with grief and loss. But now, infused with spiritual power from on high, Peter changed from a man controlled by fear to a man of great confidence and faith. Only one thing could have changed him—Pentecost—and Peter began teaching boldly in the name of Christ.

Peter had a new set of eyes with which to view life. The apostle looked quite differently on those whom he once feared when he gave the crowd prophetic knowledge:

> "Men of Israel, listen to this: Jesus of Nazareth was a man accredited by God

to you by miracles, wonders and signs, which God did among you through him, as you yourselves know. This man was handed over to you by God's set purpose and foreknowledge; and you, with the help of wicked men, put him to death by nailing him to the cross. But God raised him from the dead, freeing him from the agony of death, because it was impossible for death to keep its hold on him. . . . God has raised this Jesus to life, and we are all witnesses of the fact. Exalted to the right hand of God, he has received from the Father the promised Holy Spirit and has poured out what you now see and hear. . . . Therefore let all Israel be assured of this: God has made this Jesus, whom you crucified, both Lord and Christ."

When the people heard this, they were cut to the heart and said to Peter and the other apostles, "Brothers, what shall we do?"

Peter replied, "Repent and be baptized, every one of you, in the name of Jesus Christ for the forgiveness of your sins. And you will receive [manifest] the gift of the Holy Spirit. The promise is for you and your children and for all who are far off—for all whom the Lord our God will call." With many other words he warned them; and he pleaded with them,

"Save yourselves from this corrupt generation."

Those who accepted his message were baptized, and about three thousand were added to their number that day. (Acts 2:22–24, 32, 33, 36–41)

"Brothers, what shall we do?"

"Repent and be baptized, every one of you, in the name of Jesus Christ for the forgiveness of your sins. And you will receive the gift of the Holy Spirit."

This question and Peter's response are just as alive and real today as they were some two thousand years ago. The promises of God are unchanging.

On the first day of the "church," about three thousand people in the temple area believed Peter and received into manifestation the Holy Spirit. Imagine what could have been going through the mind of Peter. Ten days earlier, he had watched Christ ascend off the planet. Now Jerusalem was filled with the presence of Heaven, and it would soon overflow into every bloodline.

Divine intervention assured that the apostles received the inspiration they needed to carry forth what Christ had initiated on Pentecost. As documented in the Book of Acts, the apostle Peter received revelation from Heaven—in the form of a vision—directing him to take the gospel of immortality to the Gentiles. Upon his arrival at the home of a Roman soldier, Peter expounded upon the will of Heaven:

> "I now realize how true it is that God does not show favoritism but accepts men from every nation who fear [respect] him and do what is right. You know the message God sent to the people of Israel, telling the good news of peace through Jesus Christ, who is Lord of all. You know what has happened

The Divine Sign

throughout Judea, beginning in Galilee after the baptism that John preached—how God anointed Jesus of Nazareth with the Holy Spirit and power, and how he went around doing good and healing all who were under the power of the devil, because God was with him.

"We are witnesses of everything he did in the country of the Jews and in Jerusalem. They killed him by hanging him on a tree, but God raised him from the dead on the third day and caused him to be seen. He was not seen by all the people, but by witnesses whom God had already chosen—by us who ate and drank with him after he rose from the dead. He commanded us to preach to the people and to testify that he is the one whom God appointed as judge of the living and the dead. All the prophets testify about him that everyone who believes in him receives forgiveness of sins through his name."

While Peter was still speaking these words, the Holy Spirit came on all who heard the message. The circumcised

> believers who had come with Peter were astonished that the gift of the Holy Spirit had been poured out even on the Gentiles. For they heard them speaking in tongues and praising God. (Acts 10:34–46)

After Peter taught the words of Christ, the Romans manifested the sign of Christ. No one was denied entrance into the kingdom of God, and no one was denied its sign. This is the New Covenant that Christ gave to every nation, to every bloodline.

As Peter demonstrated the truth of Christ's gospel, so did the apostle Paul. When Paul visited the city of Ephesus, he taught twelve disciples about Christ's baptism, and each one spoke in tongues:

> Paul took the road through the interior and arrived at Ephesus. There he found some disciples and asked them, "Did you receive [manifest] the Holy Spirit when you believed?"
>
> They answered, "No, we have not even heard that there is a Holy Spirit."

> So Paul asked, "Then what baptism did you receive?"
>
> "John's baptism," they replied.
>
> Paul said, "John's baptism was a baptism of repentance. He told the people to believe in the one coming after him, that is, in Jesus."
>
> On hearing this, they were baptized into the name of the Lord Jesus. When Paul placed his hands on them, the Holy Spirit came on them, and they spoke in tongues and prophesied. (Acts 19:1–6)

Water baptism alone could not produce "tongues." Even John the Baptist said that his water baptism would be superceded by the spiritual baptism of Christ: "I [John] baptize you with water for repentance. But after me will come one who is more powerful than I, whose sandals I am not fit to carry. He will baptize you with the Holy Spirit and with fire" (Matt. 3:11).

This prophecy is what Paul explained to the people in the city of Ephesus, following which, all twelve had the tangible hope of a future life. The sign of Christ yielded the undeniable reality, of a personal reservation, on an Earth that is yet to be.

The truth of this great comfort has been hidden from our day and time.[2] God's supernatural sign is not reserved for only a select few within the kingdom of Christ. Divine prophecy declares, "to each one [in the kingdom of Christ] the manifestation of the Spirit is given for the common good" (1 Cor. 12:7). To each one in the kingdom is given the manifestation of the Spirit, which includes "speaking in different kinds of tongues" (1 Cor. 12:10). Speaking in new tongues is for the "common good" of Christ's kingdom on Earth.

This is why the apostle Peter exhorted the kingdom of Christ to "heed" Christ's sign, for it is the voice of God within that speaks unto Heaven: "For anyone who speaks in a tongue does not speak to men but to God. Indeed . . . he utters mysteries with his spirit. . . . in the tongues of men and of angels" (1 Cor. 14:2; 13:1).

Speaking in unknown tongues is a unique dialogue. By means of angelic and earthly languages, the kingdom of Christ can speak "divine mysteries" unto God and he "speaks" to his people through the languages that he has given. Peter's reference to Christ's transfiguration demonstrated God's presence on Earth in a different way—through different tongues.

To the kingdom of Christ the will of Heaven has been given. By revelation, the Son of God revealed it: "I would like every one of you to speak in tongues" (1 Cor. 14:5).[3] This dramatic revelation is founded upon the prophecy given by Christ himself on the day he ascended into Heaven, for at the time of the ascension, he said to his disciples: "[T]hese signs will accompany those who believe: . . . they will speak in new tongues" (Mark 16:17).

The Son of God prophesied that although he was leaving Earth, he would still be present—by way of the Holy Spirit and the sign of its indwelling presence. This prophecy—as revealed by the apostles—will continue to be fulfilled until the Son returns on the clouds of Heaven.

7

THE LIVING TEMPLE OF THE LIVING GOD

For we are the temple of the living God. As God has said: "I will live with them and walk among them, and I will be their God, and they will be my people."

—The Apostle Paul (2 Cor. 6:16)

With the New Covenant came a new temple of God, one not made of bricks and glass but of people—living stones. The sons of God—members of God's household—make up this spiritual, living temple. It is a temple that encompasses the globe; it knows no earthly boundaries.

That there would be this global temple was a mystery. It was not until the first century, when Jesus Christ gave revelation to the apostle Paul, that the fullness of this mystery was made known.

> In reading this, then, you will be able to understand my insight into the mystery of Christ, which was not made known to men in other generations as it has now been revealed by the Spirit to God's holy apostles and prophets. This mystery is that through the gospel the Gentiles are heirs together with Israel, members together of one body, and sharers together in the promise in Christ Jesus. (Eph. 3:4–6)

In this time of grace, peoples from all bloodlines can become sons of God, heirs of

Heaven, members of the living temple—"sharers together in the promise in Christ Jesus." The Old Testament prophets did not know that this would come to pass; they saw the prophecies of Christ's *suffering* and the *glory* that would (one day) follow, but they could not see the block of time that came in between: *the mystery*.

> Concerning this salvation [of souls], the [Old Testament] prophets, who spoke of the grace that was to come to you, searched intently and with the greatest care, trying to find out the time and circumstances [the mystery] to which the Spirit of Christ in them was pointing when he predicted the sufferings of Christ and the glories that would follow. (1 Peter 1:10, 11)

The prophets studied the prophecies given long before the time of Christ, yet could not assemble together all the pieces of the prophetic puzzle. This mystery was hidden, "destined for our glory before time began"

(1 Cor. 2:7). When this mystery became reality (on the day of Pentecost), the Creator initiated, and began building, his living temple on Earth—for *our* glory.

The apostles and prophets, with Christ himself being the "chief cornerstone," are the foundation of this temple:

> [Y]ou are no longer foreigners . . . but . . . members of God's household, built on the foundation of the apostles and prophets, with Christ Jesus himself as the chief cornerstone. In him the whole building is joined together and rises to become a holy temple in the Lord. And in him you too are being built together to become a dwelling in which God lives by his Spirit. (Eph. 2:19–22)

Because Christ is the chief cornerstone, the whole building is designed around and upon him. His words—the words of eternity—comprise the foundation on which the living stones are built. As given to us by Peter: "As you come to him [Jesus Christ],

The Living Temple of the Living God

the living Stone—rejected by men but chosen by God and precious to him—you also, like living stones, are being built into a spiritual house.... For in Scripture it says: 'See, I [God] lay a stone in Zion, a chosen and precious cornerstone, and the one who trusts in him will never be put to shame'" (1 Peter 2:4–6).

In his writings, Peter referenced the prophecy spoken by the Lord God, who had foretold that he would place the stone on which his spiritual temple would grow. Jesus Christ himself made reference to his words being equivalent to that of a foundation.

> [E]veryone who hears these words of mine and puts them into practice is like a wise man who built his house on the rock. The rain came down, the streams rose, and the winds blew and beat against that house; yet it did not fall, because it had its foundation on the rock. (Matt. 7:24, 25)

"The finest and noblest ground on which people can live is truth; the real with the real; a ground on which nothing is assumed."[1] Life in this world is affected by the foundation on which one chooses to build. The living temple of the living God is not only about an afterlife but also a fulfilled life.

The spiritual light that illuminates the mind and directs the heart emanates from the throne of the spiritual temple: the throne of Christ. Hence, it is to the Son of God that the sons of God look.

> Therefore, since we have a great high priest who has gone through the heavens, Jesus the Son of God, let us hold firmly to the faith we profess. For we do not have a high priest who is unable to sympathize with our weaknesses, but we have one who has been tempted in every way, just as we are—yet was without sin. Let us then approach the throne of grace with confidence, so that we may receive mercy and find grace to help us in our time of need. (Heb. 4:14–16)

The Living Temple of the Living God

This high priest in Heaven can identify with human frailty. "[W]e have one who speaks to the Father in our defense—Jesus Christ, the Righteous One" (1 John 2:1). "For through him [Christ] we both [Gentiles and Jews (i.e., all bloodlines)] have access to the Father by one Spirit" (Eph. 2:18). "For there is one God and one mediator between God and men, the man Christ Jesus" (1 Tim. 2:5). The Son of God is the intercessor between God and man. He is the living Stone on which the living stones are built, and his throne is overall.

The living stones of this spiritual temple are members of God's household and as such make up what God calls the "body of Christ." This body of believers is of spiritual design. As each part of the human body is unique and necessary for the entire body to function properly, so is the case with the spiritual "body of Christ" on Earth.

> The body is a unit, though it is made up of many parts; and though all its parts are many, they form one body. So it is with Christ. For we were all baptized by

one Spirit into one body.... Now the body [of Christ] is not made up of one part but of many. If the foot should say, "Because I am not a hand, I do not belong to the body," it would not for that reason cease to be part of the body. And if the ear should say, "Because I am not an eye, I do not belong to the body," it would not for that reason cease to be part of the body. If the whole body were an eye, where would the sense of hearing be?... But in fact God has arranged the parts in the body, every one of them, just as he wanted them to be.... God has combined the members of the body and has given greater honor to the parts that lacked it, so that there should be no division in the body, but that its parts should have equal concern for each other. If one part suffers, every part suffers with it; if one part is honored, every part rejoices with it. (1 Cor. 12:12–18, 24–26)

Now ye are the body of Christ, and members in particular. (1 Cor. 12:27 KJV)

The Living Temple of the Living God

With this analogy of the "body of Christ," Heaven reveals the individual significance of each member of the living temple. Additionally, each member plays a unique role in the overall health and well-being of the entire body of believers. The apostle Paul elaborated on how believers fulfill this role by discussing another concept: "the church" (the assembly of believers who gather for a public expression of faith).[2]

Central to the public expression of faith is the individual expression of faith: speaking in tongues. After Paul explained in his writings that all members of the "body of Christ" could manifest the Holy Spirit (1 Cor. 12:7), he switched subjects—from the "body of Christ" to "the church":

> And in the church God has appointed first of all apostles, second prophets, third teachers, then workers of miracles, also those having gifts of healing, those able to help others, those with gifts of administration, and those speaking in different kinds of tongues.

> Are all apostles? Are all prophets? Are all teachers? Do all work miracles? Do all have gifts of healing? Do all speak in tongues? Do all interpret? (1 Cor. 12:28–30)

The apostle asked a series of questions, all of which beg a "negative" response. When Paul asked, "Do all speak in tongues?" the implied answer was "no." This is the proper response to his question. However, the key to understanding Paul's line of questioning is recognizing the context within which the questions are being posed.

"Do all speak in tongues?" No, not everyone speaks in tongues—in an assembly of believers. Paul's question refers to the public expression of faith, not the individual expression of it.

Paul explained that in a public expression of faith there is to be harmony. The Spirit of Christ is to be operated in the assembly "in a fitting and orderly way" (1 Cor. 14:40)—for the strengthening of the assembly.

The Living Temple of the Living God

> All of these must be done for the strengthening of the church. If anyone speaks in a tongue, two—or at the most three—should speak, one at a time, and someone must interpret. (1 Cor. 14:26, 27)

In the assembly, two or three believers bring forth the sign of tongues and the corresponding interpretation. According to the apostle Paul, the one who speaks in tongues is the one who interprets: "[A]nyone who speaks in a tongue should pray that he may interpret what he says" (1 Cor. 14:13). Each believer "interprets [the tongue], so that the church may be edified [built up]" (1 Cor. 14:5). Heaven has empowered the kingdom of Christ to speak in divinely inspired languages and interpret them, so that the living temple may receive divinely inspired words from the Spirit of Christ within.

Christ himself said: "[W]here two or three come together in my name, there am I with them" (Matt. 18:20). It is with this spiritual picture in mind that we identify with the simplicity and beauty of "tongues" and their "interpretation." When two or three gather in the name of Christ, *he is present*, and the supernatural manifestation of his presence is made known by way of speaking in tongues and their interpretation. That is their design.

It is by way of the Spirit of Christ that "tongues" are spoken forth, and it is by way of that same Spirit that the language is interpreted (explained). The apostle Paul said the interpretation of the "tongue" becomes a reality by way of *prayer*. "Pray" that you may be able to interpret your God-given "tongues," and it shall become your reality—you shall speak it forth.

What separates Christianity from all other religions is the Spirit of Christ, and it is by way of that Spirit, that Christ "speaks" to those *within* his temple and to those *not yet within* the temple, for "tongues . . . are a sign, not for believers but for unbelievers" (1 Cor. 14:22). The sign of Christ is the light of Christ. It illuminates where there is darkness, so that souls not yet illuminated ("unbelievers") can "see" the reality of the Spirit of Christ and be liberated from Satan's deception.

Look at the picture Christ first gave to Paul when he appeared to him: "I [Christ] am sending you to them to open their eyes and turn them from darkness to light, and from the power of Satan to God, so that they may receive forgiveness of sins and a place among those who are sanctified by faith in me" (Acts 26:17, 18). Instrumental in bringing this to pass was the sign of Christ—which Paul taught and wrote about.

As Paul states, manifesting Christ's sign is an individual expression of faith and one of the *nine* manifestations of the Holy Spirit. The manifestations are as follows:

> But the manifestation of the Spirit is given to every man to profit withal. For to one is given by the Spirit the word of wisdom; to another the word of knowledge by the same Spirit; To another faith by the same Spirit; to another the gifts of healing by the same Spirit; To another

> the working of miracles; to another prophecy; to another discerning of spirits; to another *divers* kinds of tongues; to another the interpretation of tongues: But all these worketh that one and the selfsame Spirit, dividing to every man [in the temple] severally as he [the Spirit] will. (1 Cor. 12:7–11 KJV)

The Spirit determines the total number of manifestations that a believer will manifest. However, in the case of speaking in tongues, the Spirit has already determined that every member of the living temple can know the reality of it (1 Cor. 14:5). The determination of who can speak in tongues is not a *present* tense decision of the Spirit; it is a *past* tense decision that believers bring forth "tongues." (This is not to say that speaking in a tongue is a prerequisite to attain eternal life; the sign of "tongues" is the evidence that eternal life has already been attained.)

Wherever you are in your spiritual journey, the sign of "tongues" is meant to establish the heart. Manifesting Christ's sign yields

The Living Temple of the Living God 247

an inner strengthening for the individual stones of the temple. "He who speaks in a tongue edifies [builds up] himself" (1 Cor. 14:4). "Therefore, my brothers . . . do not forbid speaking in tongues" (1 Cor. 14:39). "[W]hat I am writing to you is the Lord's command" (1 Cor. 14:37).

It is important to note the following: when Paul introduces speaking in tongues, he defines it not as a "gift" (Greek: *charisma*) but as a "manifestation" (Greek: *phanerosis*). These distinct concepts—*charisma* and *phanerosis*—fall under the overall umbrella of *pneumatikos*, which refers to matters of the Holy Spirit.[3] By revelation, the Son of God revealed to his kingdom that only one manifestation is a gift: healing.

All nine manifestations are unique, supernatural forms of manifesting the presence of Heaven on Earth. Examples of the manifestations can be found throughout the Book of Acts—which gives the kingdom of Christ a glimpse into the first century A.D., and reveals the magnitude of divine intervention within the living temple.

The Son of God—from his throne in Heaven—gave revelation to the apostles so that the living stones of the spiritual temple would have a defined understanding of their place in this life—confident of Heaven's will. As given to us by the apostle John: "Beloved, I wish above all things that thou mayest prosper and be in health, even as thy soul prospereth" (3 John 2 KJV). The health of the physical body, the "life" of the soul, and prosperity and strengthening of all in the temple represent fulfillment. It is what Heaven seeks for the sons of God—a life founded upon the rock of all ages: Christ Jesus.

> The thief [Satan] cometh not, but for to steal, and to kill, and to destroy: I am come that they might have life, and that they might have *it* more abundantly.
>
> —The Son of God (John 10:10 KJV)

8

CROWNS AND GLORY

> For the Son of Man is going to come in his Father's glory with his angels, and then he will reward each person according to what he has done.
>
> —The Son of God (Matt. 16:27)

When the Son of God descends from above to gather his kingdom, the floodgates of Heaven's wealth shall open. The immortal souls that ascend off the planet shall awaken to spiritual abundance when they stand in the presence of Christ. For, from the throne of Christ—the judgment seat—the King of kings and Lord of lords will judge the righteous souls, determining the impartation of his "reward."

> For we must all appear before the judgment seat of Christ, that each one may receive what is due him for the things done while in the body, whether good or bad. (2 Cor. 5:10)

"Good" things refer to actions of the heart that are worthy of admiration; "bad" things express a lack of moral character, unbefitting for someone who claims to represent the Son of God. The Messiah is not unrighteous to forget what has been accomplished "in the [physical] body."

Christ will remember where his love flowed on Earth; it is the standard by which he will judge—it is the commandment that he gave: "A new command I give you: Love one another. As I have loved you, so you must love one another. By this all men will know that you are my disciples, if you love one another" (John 13:34, 35).[1]

Living life based on divine love produces not only divine actualization in this life but also the promise of prophecy being personally applied in the next. Earth is a staging area for all future events; life in this world shall profoundly affect the hereafter. Salvation is by grace, but reward is by merit.

Yet everyone who made Jesus "Lord" shall be honored; none who stand before Christ shall be condemned, for the blood of the Lamb already removed all condemnation. Hence, the appearance before the judgment seat of Christ, "has nothing to do with justification, which is credited to the Christian fully and forever through faith in Christ; instead, it refers to what we have done with our lives as Christians."[2]

While teaching in the Holy Land, the Messiah made reference to this future point in time when he spoke of "treasure." He said that the accumulation of it is directly contingent on the heart. Where it is determines the harvest.

> Now when he [Jesus] saw the crowds, he went up on a mountainside and sat down. His disciples came to him, and he began to teach them, saying: . . . "[S]tore up for yourselves treasures in heaven, where moth and rust do not destroy, and where thieves do not break in and steal. For where your treasure is, there your heart will be also." (Matt. 5:1, 2; 6:20, 21)

To his followers, Jesus taught the following: to pursue the will of Heaven is to obtain the wealth of Heaven. He presented the logic of applying one's heart to attain eternal glory, for material gain of this world cannot hide from the simple fact that it is temporal. The greatest earthly wealth cannot outdistance time. "For what is seen is temporary, but what is unseen is eternal" (2 Cor. 4:18).

The everlasting Lord revealed this invisible world of spiritual treasures by way of revelation to his disciples. The writings of Peter, James, John, and Paul, reveal a picture of Heaven's deepest riches: the eternal crowns. Christ the King shall "crown" righteous souls in his kingdom with "life," "glory," and "righteousness." Each of these "qualities" represents "crowns" of everlasting heavenly honor, and Christ shall bestow these crowns, based on what is accomplished in the name of Heaven. As recorded in the letter written by James:

> Blessed is the man who perseveres under trial, because when he has stood the test, he will receive the crown of life that God has promised to those who love him. When tempted, no one should say, "God is tempting me." For God cannot be tempted by evil, nor does he tempt anyone; but each one is tempted when, by his own evil desire, he is dragged away and enticed. . . . Every good and perfect gift is from above, coming down from the Father of the heavenly lights, who does not change like shifting shadows. (James 1:12–14, 17)

Our faithfulness to our God includes rejecting the notion that he would tempt his own children. In the Garden of Eden, Satan, not God, did the tempting. "God is light; in him there is no darkness at all" (1 John 1:5). The Almighty is absolute light; therefore, temptation is darkness.

God fixed the light in the sky to demonstrate his order and faithfulness in creation. His will doesn't shift as shadows upon Earth. He is the giver of "good and perfect gifts." He is not the source of tribulation upon the righteous; he is the source of comfort:

> Blessed *be* God, even the Father of our Lord Jesus Christ, the Father of mercies, and the God of all comfort; Who comforteth us in all our tribulation, that we may be able to comfort them which are in any trouble, by the comfort wherewith we ourselves are comforted of God. (2 Cor. 1:3, 4 KJV)

"[T]he Lord watches over the way of the righteous" (Ps. 1:6). As written by King David:

"I sought the Lord, and he answered me; he delivered me from all my fears" (Ps. 34:4). Freeing the soul from anchors of internal pressure is what the God of comfort seeks for his people, and a crown of life awaits those souls who respond to this God of love with an unwavering mind-set.

No clearer example of faithfulness can be found on Earth than Jesus Christ. To study his life is to study the wisdom of the ages, for within him was the word of truth. He showed mankind—by example—the meaning and purpose of life. Together with his apostles, he demonstrated the impact of giving the truth to those who seek it.

Following his Resurrection, Jesus met with his apostles and spoke to this very subject. His closing words dealt with his kingdom and the edifying of it. To the apostle Peter, Jesus asked, "'Simon [Peter] son of John, do you truly love me?' He answered, 'Yes, Lord, you know that I love you.' Jesus said, 'Take care of my sheep'" (John 21:16). The significance of these words cannot be underestimated, for to assimilate the word of truth is to feed the mind with life.

Years after this conversation with Jesus, Peter wrote about it, declaring that the "crown of glory" awaits those who impart the truth.

> Be shepherds of God's flock that is under your care, serving as overseers—not because you must, but because you are willing, as God wants you to be; not greedy for money, but eager to serve; not lording it over those entrusted to you, but being examples to the flock. And when the Chief Shepherd appears, you will receive the crown of glory that will never fade away. (1 Peter 5:2–4)

As with Peter, each one in the kingdom holds a unique place in God's mind. Likewise each one can have a unique impact on the hearts and minds of those within one's sphere of influence. It is the calling of Heaven to respond with the love that God places in the heart, nurturing and comforting with the

Crowns and Glory 257

truth. Only truth can make one free and only the Lord can divinely recognize those who gave the truth and lived it.

When the Chief Shepherd returns to Earth, he shall crown his flock not only with "life" and "glory" but also with "righteousness." This third crown is destined for those who kept in their heart the faith given by their Lord. As recorded by the apostle Paul:

> I have fought the good fight, I have finished the race, I have kept the faith. Now there is in store for me the crown of righteousness, which the Lord, the righteous Judge, will award to me on that day—and not only to me, but also to all who have longed for his appearing. (2 Tim. 4:7, 8)

No amount of negative energy could stop Paul from wielding the sword of the Spirit (the Word of God). He lived his life in the name of truth, slicing through the spiritual darkness that pervaded the world in the first century. He held to the will of God and derived strength from his fixed mindset. He had the absolute assurance that his Lord would remember him and all in the kingdom, which lived for the unseen, greater good. To this end, Paul said:

> Command those who are rich in this present world . . . to put their hope in God, who richly provides us with everything for our enjoyment. Command them to do good, to be rich in good deeds, and to be generous and willing to share. In this way they will lay up treasure for themselves as a firm foundation for the coming age, so that they may take hold of the life that is truly life. (1 Tim. 6:17–19)

What is life that is "truly life"? Ask this question a hundred times and it could yield a hundred different answers. Yet, according to Heaven, life that is truly life is found in perceiving mortal existence in light of eternal realities. To store up treasures in Heaven is to embrace the spiritual reality of this world and the next. To view one's self in light of the "coming age," is to arrive at new plateaus in one's walk with God. Knowledge of the truth is empowering; seeking to gain it and apply it far exceeds any other answer to the question: What is life?

We only have one soul, one life, with which to live in this world of finite time. "No eternal reward will forgive us now for wasting the dawn."[3] Clearly, anything that is counterproductive to God cannot yield Heaven's blessing in the future world. We need only apply logic and love in response to divine prophecy, for if the second coming of Christ shall unveil all that currently waits in Heaven, then the only reasonable response is to live for it.

As written by the apostle Paul: "[W]hat *is* our hope, or joy, or crown of rejoicing? *Are* not even ye in the presence of our Lord Jesus Christ at his coming?" (1 Thess. 2:19 KJV). Paul said his "crown of rejoicing" would be all the immortal souls who stand with him in the presence of Christ the King.

The hope and the joy of Heaven is that the righteous of God shall know the treasures of God forever. Until this glorious day dawns, "The Lord bless you and keep you; the Lord make his face shine upon you and be gracious to you; the Lord turn his face toward you and give you peace" (Num. 6:24–26).

Epilogue

Modern-day Psalms

At age 12, I was a fan of [King] David, he felt familiar . . . like a pop star could feel familiar. The words of the psalms were as poetic as they were religious and he was a star. . . . Years ago, . . . we were still looking for a song to close our third album, *War*. . . . We thought about the psalms. . . . "Psalm 40" is interesting in that it suggests a time in which grace will replace karma, and love replace the very strict laws of Moses (i.e. fulfill them). I love that thought.

—bono, U2

"'40' became the closing song at U2 shows and on hundreds of occasions, literally hundreds of thousands of people of every size and shape t-shirt have shouted back the refrain, pinched from 'Psalm 6': 'How long' (to sing this song)".[1]

The intrigue regarding the Creator doesn't stop with divine revelation delivered by the biblical prophets. This eternal intelligence also has communicated with Earth in ways that are not stereotyped as "biblical" but clearly are "spiritual."

God's communication on Earth is not limited to a particular classification of "religious" settings; there are no man-made categorizations that this intelligence must function within. God doesn't impart knowledge or judge based on titles or institutions, for "the Lord looketh on the heart" (1 Sam. 16:7 KJV).

The essence of this discussion is that God is within the kingdoms of men and he inspires whom he chooses. He is everywhere present, unlimited by time or space and certainly not held captive by the traditions of men.

I would like to turn your attention back to where this Epilogue started: music. Music is a powerful venue for communicating thoughts and ideas. It fills our soul with energy, and it can heal the heart; we find ourselves in the message. Music can inspire, enlighten, or incite.

With this backdrop, we'll look at a unique year in time: 1967. The summer of 1967 is now known as the "summer of love." "God is love" (1 John 4:16). I submit to you that the God of Heaven inspired the "summer of love."

That year opened up with the release of The Doors' first record. One song on the album is "Light My Fire."[2] Although it contains obvious references to sexuality, a much more intriguing picture emerges when viewed through the eyes of band member Ray Manzarek. In an interview with *Revolver* magazine, he stated: "My God, 'Light My Fire' had the magic in it. Robby [Krieger] was blessed, just like how in the Bible the Holy Ghost comes and blesses Jesus' disciples and a little tongue of flame descends upon all of their heads. A tongue of flame descended upon Robby's head when he wrote 'Light My Fire.'"[3]

Described here is a picture of inspiration. If Heaven inspired King David to write "songs" in the Psalms, then why couldn't Heaven inspire songs for our generation? The presence of a "tongue of fire" yields a fascinating conclusion: there are spiritual connotations to "Light My Fire." While pondering this concept, we can consider the following: "[T]he Lord thy God *is* a consuming fire" (Deut. 4:24 KJV), and fire is a sign of his presence (Acts 2:3).

To add further intrigue to this story, The Doors' first album finds Jim Morrison singing, "Save us! Jesus! Save us!" When he sang this, he did so as a spiritual poet.

Consider the poets John Lennon and Paul McCartney, and the inspiration that produced The Beatles' song: "All You Need Is Love."[4] "One of the most celebrated pop singles ever, this anthem for love was broadcast virtually as it was recorded—live—in Our World, the first global TV programme, seen by satellite over much of the planet on June 25 1967."[5] "All You Need Is Love" is forever linked to opening the "summer of love."

In separate interviews on the subject of spirituality, Lennon said: "Studying religion has made me try to improve relationships, not to be unpleasant. It's not a conscious move to change my personality. I'm just trying to be how I want to be, and how I'd like others to be."[6] "I don't profess to be a practicing christian . . . but I think Christ was what he was, and if anybody says anything great about him, I believe."[7]

On being a composer Lennon once said: "I've had one or two things up my sleeve, I was going to make recordings of some of my poetry. But I'm not high powered. I just sort of stand there and let things happen to me."[8]

The greatest cargos of life come over quiet seas; a peaceful mind that has the right "heart" can receive and produce love that affects the way we view the world, the future, and ourselves.

What do we take away from all of this? To think of the Creator not as an entity that is elsewhere, but here, within so many of us—inspiring people on this planet to communicate the nature of Heaven.

To look to the source of love sets in motion divine events that impact the energy within our souls, and thereby on Earth. The things we do in love will be remembered. Let us embrace our heavenly Father, his creation, and the apex of that creation: us.

It is my prayer that your vision—for your life—has been enhanced.

I welcome you to further explore the subject of divine revelation, and invite you to contact me by visiting my Website at: *www.thetimeline.org*.

May the Lord bless you and keep you in his perfect peace.

NOTES

PROLOGUE: CREATION: THEORY AND PROPHECY

1. Douglas J. Futuyma, *Science on Trial: The Case for Evolution* (New York: Pantheon Books, 1983), 197. Available http://www.pathlights.com. "Scientists Speak about Evolution." Retrieval date: 17 December 2001.

2. Michael Denton, *Evolution: A Theory in Crisis* (Chevy Chase, Md.: Adler & Adler Publishers, Inc., 1986), 67. Available http://www.pathlights.com. "Scientists Speak about Evolution." Retrieval date: 17 December 2001.

3. Adrian Desmond, "Darwin: The Man and His Legacy." Available http://www.bbc.co.uk/education/darwin/leghist/desmond.htm. Retrieval date: 17 December 2001.

4. Charles Darwin, *The Origin of Species*, Chapter 14: Recapitulation and Conclusion. Available http://www.literature.org/author/darwin-charles/the-origin-of-species/chapter-14.html. Retrieval date: 31 May 2002.

5. The English translation of Genesis 1:2 reads, "the earth was without form, and void." However, the Hebrew word for "was" is not "to be" but is literally "to become," E.W. Bullinger, *The Companion Bible* (Grand Rapids, Mich.: Kregel Publications, 1990), 3.

Hence, the translation needs to be "became without form, and void."

6. D. B. Gower, "Scientist Rejects Evolution," *Kentish (England) Times*, 11 December 1975. Available http://www.pathlights.com. "Scientists Speak about Evolution." Retrieval date: 17 December 2001.

7. *Creation: The Cutting Edge—Acts, Facts, Impacts* (1982), 26. Available http://www.pathlights.com. "Scientists Speak about Evolution." Retrieval date: 17 December 2001.

8. Denton, *Evolution: A Theory in Crisis*, 77.

9. Sean Henahan, "Neanderthal: No Relation," 10 July 1997. Available: http://www.accessexcellence.org/WN/SUA10/neander797.html. Retrieval date: 6 May 2003.

10. Michael J. Behe, "Darwin under the Microscope," *The New York Times*, 29 October 1996, Tuesday Final, sec. A. Available http://www.arn.org/docs/behe/mb_dm11496.htm. Retrieval date: 17 December 2001.

11. Adrian Desmond and James Moore, *Darwin* (New York: W. W. Norton and Company, 1991), 456. Available http://www.creationdigest.com/CanYouBelieve.htm. Retrieval date: 9 October 2002.

12. L. Merson Davies, *Modern Science*, 1953. Available http://www.pathlights.com. "Scientists Speak about Evolution." Retrieval date: 17 December 2001.

13. Colin Patterson, "Darwin, Evolution, Natural Selection," 23 July 1999. Available http://www.tdtone.org/darwin/Index.html. Retrieval date: 17 December 2001.

14. John Patrick Michael Murphy, "Charles Darwin (1999)." Available http://

www.infidels.org/library/modern/ john_murphy/charlesdarwin.html. Retrieval date: 17 December 2001.

15. Andrew Chaikin, "Are There Other Universes?" 5 February 2002. Available http://www.space.com. Retrieval date: 5 February 2002.

16. William C. Mitchel, "Big Bang Theory under Fire," Physics Essays (vol. 10, no. 2), June 1997. Available http://nowscape.com/big-ban2.htm. Retrieval date: 4 February 2002.

17. Andrew Chaikin, "Dark Energy: Astronomers Still 'Clueless' about Mystery Force Pushing Galaxies Apart," 15 January 2002. Available http://www.space.com. Retrieval date: 4 February 2002.

18. Ibid.

19. Ibid.

20. Robert Roy Britt, "The Big Rip: New Theory Ends Universe by Shredding Everything," 6 March 2003. Available http://www.space.com. Retrieval date: 6 March 2003.

21. Britt, "'Groundbreaking' Discovery: First Observation of Dark Matter."

22. Robert Roy Britt, "Understanding Dark Matter and Light Energy," 5 January 2001. Available http://www.space.com. Retrieval date: 23 January 2002.

23. Britt, "'Groundbreaking' Discovery: First Observation of Dark Matter."

24. Ibid.

25. Ibid.

26. Mitchel, "Big Bang Theory under Fire."

27. Eric J. Lerner, *The Big Bang Never Happened* (New York: Vintage Books, 1992), 4.

28. Chaikin, "Dark Energy: Astronomers Still 'Clueless' about Mystery Force Pushing Galaxies Apart."

29. John Fulton, "A New Chronology." Available: http://www.freerepublic.com/forum/a368da48f3b90.htm. Retrieval date: 22 June 2003.

30. Of notable importance are artifacts that relate to Moses: the founding father of monotheism—the belief in the one and only God. Throughout the twentieth century, archaeologists searched for evidence that would shed light on this story of Moses and the exodus (the Israelite journey out of Egypt to the Holy Land).

Recently, an archaeological find gave credibility to a record that pertains to the exodus: the story of Pharaoh's charioteers pursuing the escaping Israelites. The narrative states that as Moses led the children of Israel across the Egyptian landscape, Pharaoh had a change of heart regarding the exodus. "So he [Pharaoh] had his chariot made ready and took his army with him. He took six hundred of the best chariots, along with all the other chariots of Egypt. . . . [And] he pursued the Israelites" (Exod. 14:6–8). Of the chariots that raced after the Israelites, the "six hundred" were considered to be Pharaoh's personal chariots.

Recently, on an archeological dig in the site of Pharaoh's capital, German archaeologists discovered a tethering stone (used to secure a horse) and found a hubcap for a chariot wheel. Once fully excavated, the site revealed enough stables to house nearly 500 hundred horses and chariots. Therewith, archaeologists provided evidence that the large number of chariots described in the Book of Exodus could not be dismissed as impossible.

31. "Who is Jesus?" Available http://www.whoisJesus-really.com. Retrieval date: 20 January 2002.

1. SPIRITUAL WARFARE

1. "Now is the judgment of this world: now shall the prince of this world [Satan] be cast out" (John 12:31 KJV).

2. EVENTS OF THE END: THE SEVEN SEALS OF CHRIST'S PROPHECY

1. This revelation given by Christ in Mark 13 is in contextual sequence (not chronological order). The signs of Christ's return—although they follow the time of the Antichrist in the narrative (Mark 13:14–27)—actually precede the time of the Antichrist in terms of the order of events.

The revelation given in Mark 13 corresponds to the questions asked by the apostles. The first question in the Gospel of Mark addressed when the temple stones would be thrown down, and the second question was as follows: "And what will be the sign that they are all about to be fulfilled?" Hence, when Jesus referred to the signs, he referred to the apostles' second question—a time that precedes "the abomination that causes desolation" (when the stones will be thrown down). The signs correspond to the time that follows the "distress" of the "birth pains" (spoken of earlier).

In essence, the revelation given by Jesus in the Gospel of Mark is in relation to the specific line of questioning; it does not reflect a progression of events on an unbroken continuum. This is why the order of events in Mark appears to be opposite the numbered chronology set forth by John in the Book of Revelation.

2. "The great tribulation" ends with the sixth seal, and the "day of wrath" commences after the seventh seal. It is evident that Christians will face tribulation from evil in this world (John 16:33 KJV), but the apostle Paul stated that those who are sealed by Spirit are excluded from God's future wrath (1 Thess. 1:10). "Tribulation" affects the righteous but "wrath" never will. Hence, "tribulation" and "wrath" represent mutually exclusive expressions.

3. E. W. Bullinger, *A Critical Lexicon and Concordance to the English and Greek New Testament* (Grand Rapids, Mich.: Zondervan Publishing House, 1981), 832.

4. *New International Version Study Bible* (Grand Rapids, Mich.: Zondervan Publishing House, 1995), 1830.

5. *New Illustrated Bible Dictionary* (Nashville, Tenn.: Thomas Nelson Publishers, 1995), 818.

6. Robert L. Thomas, *Revelation 8–22, An Exegetical Commentary* (Chicago: Moody Press, 1995), 585.

7. *New International Version Study Bible*, 1577.

3. THE SEVENTIETH "SEVEN"

1. The seventieth "seven" applies not to the "church of the living God" (1 Tim. 3:15), but to Daniel's "people" (Dan. 9:24)—the twelve tribes from which Daniel was born.

4. THE CODE OF PSALMS

1. E. W. Bullinger, *The Companion Bible* (Grand Rapids, Mich.: Kregel Publications, 1990), 720.

2. J. R. Church, *Hidden Prophecies in the Psalms* (Oklahoma City, Okla.: Prophecy Publications, 1990), 300.

3. One general observation that can be made regarding the Book of Psalms as it pertains to the nation of Israel is its location in the Bible: it is the nineteenth book (counting forward from Genesis) and it is the forty-eighth book (counting backward from Revelation). Herein, the chronological location of the Psalms offers relevance to the birth date of Israel.

4. Church, *Hidden Prophecies in the Psalms,* 151.

5. James Strong, *Abingdon's Strong's Exhaustive Concordance of the Bible* (Nashville,

Tenn.: Abingdon, 1981), 11 (Hebrew and Chaldee Dictionary).

6. The Hebrew word for "next" is *acher*, which means "following," James Strong, *Abingdon's Strong's Exhaustive Concordance of the Bible* (Nashville, Tenn.: Abingdon, 1981), 11 (Hebrew and Chaldee Dictionary). Hence, "next generation" refers to the "generation that follows."

5. THE DOORS OF PARADISE

1. According to Jesus and Moses, paradise is not a place in Heaven but on Earth. Moses spoke of the first paradise where the tree of life stood, and Jesus spoke of the future paradise (which is the new Earth), where the tree of life will once again stand. This is the paradise Jesus promised to the condemned man. With a verbal exclamation mark, he said, "I tell you the truth today! You will be with me in [the future] paradise."

2. *New Illustrated Bible Dictionary* (Nashville, Tenn.: Thomas Nelson Publishers, 1995), 894.

3. After the Messiah's blood cleanses sin, the righteousness of God cannot be lost because the Spirit of Christ created within is righteous. Yet, in our walk with God, human frailty can produce the need for forgiveness. New Testament prophecy addresses this by directing us to go to Heaven in prayer: "Let us then approach the throne of grace with confidence, so that we may receive mercy and find grace to help us in our time of need" (Heb. 4:16). Whether seeking forgiveness or fulfillment of an earnest prayer, "the effectual fervent prayer of a righteous man availeth much" (James 5:16 KJV).

6. THE DIVINE SIGN

1. The key to understanding "receive the Holy Spirit" is found in the definition of the Greek word *lambano*, which is translated into the English word "receive." *Lambano* denotes

receiving an object to the end of displaying its presence.

The Greek word literally means "to take what is given . . . pointing to an objective reception," E. W. Bullinger, *A Critical Lexicon and Concordance to the English and Greek New Testament* (Grand Rapids, Mich.: Zondervan Publishing House, 1981), 626.

When the Lord and his apostles said, "receive the Holy Spirit," they referred to objectively receiving it in the form of manifesting Christ's sign of tongues. "*Lambano* the Holy Spirit" is synonymous with "manifest the Holy Spirit."

2. Paul's first letter to the Corinthians was written c. 55. Approximately twelve years later, Paul wrote the following words to Timothy (a trusted leader): "You know that everyone in the province of Asia has deserted me" (2 Tim. 1:15). Herein, long before the end of the first century A.D., the apostle Paul witnessed countless numbers of believers abandon the revelation that had been given to him by Jesus Christ.

Parallel to this thought is what the apostle John wrote in his third letter: "I wrote to the church, but Diotrephes, who loves to be first, will have nothing to do with us. So if I come, I will call attention to what he is doing, gossiping maliciously about us. Not satisfied with that, he refuses to welcome the brothers. He also stops those who want to do so and puts them out of the church" (3 John 9, 10).

John revealed the mindset of a church leader so twisted that he rejected not only an apostle but also cast Christ's followers out of the church. Herein, looking back twenty centuries, we know that there was a rejection of John and Paul and the sound doctrine they taught.

To establish this thought, we need only look to the revelation given by Jesus Christ to the apostle John. As the first century A.D. drew to a close, Christ addressed the following words to church representatives in Asia Minor: "You have forsaken your first love" (Rev. 2:4); "I know your deeds; you have a reputation of being alive, but you are dead. Wake up! Strengthen what remains and is about to die, for I have not found your deeds complete in the sight of my God" (Rev. 3:1, 2).

Bringing together the words of Christ, John, and Paul, an unsettling picture emerges: spirituality at the end of the first century had been negatively affected. If all of Asia had turned away from the apostle Paul and church leadership refused access to the apostle John and Christ said that "deeds" were incomplete, we can only conclude that there was a forsaking of Heaven's doctrine—which includes teaching and speaking the sign of Christ. This glorious manifestation—given to the church by Christ—was swept away by those who had forsaken John and Paul.

3. The first sentence of 1 Corinthians 14:5 reads as follows: "I would like every one of you to speak in tongues, but I would rather have you prophesy." Paul refers to two of the manifestations: "tongues" and "prophesy." Whereas "tongues" is an individual expression

of faith designed for the individual believer, "prophesy" is a public expression of faith designed for the assembly of believers. Paul states that he'd rather have a believer prophesy because of the greater impact on "the church," but it does not negate the truth concerning speaking in tongues—that of Paul's desire that all believers in the "body of Christ" speak forth the sign of Christ to benefit their individual walk with God.

7. THE LIVING TEMPLE OF THE LIVING GOD

1. Ralph Waldo Emerson, "Quotable Quotes." Available: http://www.quotablequotes.net/. Retrieval date: 15 December 2002.

2. In the New Testament, the word "church" denotes the "redeemed community." Although "church" can mean the entire world community that calls upon Christ, it can also refer to a smaller "block" of the living temple: "every Church in which the

character of the Church as a whole is seen in miniature," E. W. Bullinger, *A Critical Lexicon and Concordance to the English and Greek New Testament* (Grand Rapids, Mich.: Zondervan Publishing House, 1981), 153.

3. Paul's discussion on *pneumatikos* begins with the following: "Now concerning spiritual *gifts*, brethren, I would not have you ignorant (1 Cor. 12:1 KJV)." The Greek word for "spiritual" is *pneumatikos*. The word "gifts" is in italics because there is no corresponding Greek word for "gifts" in the Greek text. Hence, *pneumatikos* is the concept that governs the progression of thought that follows in Paul's letter. In essence, matters belonging to the Holy Spirit are presented in various forms: *phanerosis* of Christ's sign is one form and *charisma* represents another.

8. CROWNS AND GLORY

1. Jesus Christ communicated that the perfection of the Old Testament Law is fulfilled by following New Testament love:

"'Love the Lord your God with all your heart and with all your soul and with all your mind.' This is the first and greatest commandment. And the second is like it: 'Love your neighbor as yourself.' All the Law and the Prophets hang on these two commandments" (Matt. 22:37–39).

2. *New International Version Study Bible* (Grand Rapids, Mich.: Zondervan Publishing House, 1995), 1769.

3. *Jim Morrison: The Doors: Live in Europe: 1968,* New York: Doors Music Company, 58 min., 1988, videocassette.

EPILOGUE

1. Selections from the Book of Psalms (New York: Grove Press, 1999), vii, xi.

2. The Doors, *The Doors*, Elektra/Asylum Records, 1988.

3. Alan Paul, "The Doors of Perception," *Revolver*, Premiere Issue, 75.

4. The Beatles, *Magical Mystery Tour*, Capitol Records, 1967.

5. "The Beatles." Available: http://beatles.com/html/allyouneedislove/. Retrieval date: 6 June 2003.

6. "The Beatles Ultimate Experience." Available: http://www.geocities.com/beatleboy1_99/db67.html. Retrieval date: 18 June 2003.

7. "The Beatles Ultimate Experience." Available:http://www.geocities.com/beatleboy1_99/db66.html. Retrieval date: 18 June 2003.

8. "John Lennon, NME.com." Available: http://microsites.nme.com/lennon/site/features2.html. Retrieval date: 18 June 2003.

PSALM 103

A Psalm of David

Praise the Lord, O my soul; all my inmost being, praise his holy name.

Praise the Lord, O my soul, and forget not all his benefits—who forgives all your sins and heals all your diseases, who redeems your life from the pit and crowns you with love and compassion, who satisfies your desires with good things so that your youth is renewed like the eagle's. The Lord works righteousness and justice for all the oppressed.

He made known his ways to Moses, his deeds to the people of Israel:

The Lord is compassionate and gracious, slow to anger, abounding in love.

He will not always accuse, nor will he harbor his anger forever; he does not treat us as our sins deserve or repay us according to our iniquities.

For as high as the heavens are above the earth, so great is his love for those who fear him; as far as the east is from the west, so far has he removed our transgressions from us.

As a father has compassion on his children, so the Lord has compassion on those who fear him; for he knows how we are formed, he remembers that we are dust.

As for man, his days are like grass, he flourishes like a flower of the field; the wind blows over it and it is gone, and its place remembers it no more.

But from everlasting to everlasting the Lord's love is with those who fear him, and his righteousness with their children's children—with those who keep his covenant and remember to obey his precepts. The Lord has established his throne in heaven, and his kingdom rules over all. Praise the Lord, you his angels, you mighty ones who do his bidding, who obey his word.

Praise the Lord, all his heavenly hosts, you his servants who do his will.

Praise the Lord, all his works everywhere in his dominion.

Praise the Lord, O my soul.

Acknowledgments

When writing a book, it helps to have a saint in your life who is your continual source of inspiration. That is why my heartfelt thankfulness goes to Vera, my sweetheart.

I learned most about faith from my parents and grandparents, and to them goes my deepest gratitude. From my sister Linda and brother Stephen, I received unending support, and to each I extend a prayer of thanks.

I wish to acknowledge my enduring appreciation for the friend who was with me from inception to completion of this publication: Mike Rufini. His knowledge of Scripture and faithfulness combined to produce assistance that was essential in bringing about the finished product. I also am indebted to another good friend of mine, Jeff Mayfield, for his informed input.

Finally, I am grateful for the followers of Christ who have gone before me, Christians who believed and taught the apostles' doctrine, and contributed to the body of scriptural knowledge from which I was privileged to draw.

Acknowledgments 297

Front Cover Description:
A photograph from NASA's Hubble Space Telescope displays the "eerie, wispy tendrils of a dark interstellar cloud being destroyed by the passage of one of the brightest stars in the Pleiades star cluster. Like a flashlight beam shining off the wall of a cave, the star is reflecting light off the surface of pitch black clouds of cold gas laced with dust. These are called reflection nebulae." Available http://heritage.stsci.edu/2000/36/table.html

Back Cover Description:
Photograph of the constellation "Orion."
Photo from Bill and Sally Fletcher: Available http://www.scienceandart.com/photoorionconst.htm

TIMELINE INTERNATIONAL logo photo:
NASA photograph: Spiral Galaxy NGC 4622.
Available: http://heritage.stsci.edu/2002/03/index.html

The "Pleiades" and "Orion" were spoken of by Old Testament prophets (Job 9:9; 38:31; and Amos 5:8).

To order additional copies of

THE
PROPHECY

Call TIMELINE INTERNATIONAL @ (860) 680-9000

Or order online @ www.thetimeline.org

Or send $12.00* each plus $4.00 S&H** to

TIMELINE INTERNATIONAL
PO Box 914
South Windsor, CT 06074

*Connecticut residents, add 6% sales tax
**Add $2.00 S&H for each additional book ordered